Drew Provan

iPhone

covers iOS 9

6th edition

updated for iPhone 6s and 6s Plus

In easy steps is an imprint of In Easy Steps Limited
16 Hamilton Terrace · Holly Walk · Leamington Spa
Warwickshire · United Kingdom · CV32 4LY
www.ineasysteps.com

Sixth Edition

Notice of Liability
Every effort has been made to ensure that this book contains accurate
and current information. However, In Easy Steps Limited and the
author shall not be liable for any loss or damage suffered by readers
as a result of any information contained herein.

Trademarks
All trademarks are acknowledged as belonging to their respective
companies.

In Easy Steps Limited supports The Forest Stewardship Council (FSC),
the leading international forest certification organization. All our titles
that are printed on Greenpeace approved FSC certified paper carry the
FSC logo.

MIX
Paper from
responsible sources
FSC® C020837

Printed and bound in the United Kingdom

ISBN 978-1-84078-707-8

Contents

10 Email   159

11 Accessibility Settings   169

12 Solving Problems   177

Index   187

1 The iPhone 6s and iPhone 6s Plus

The latest iPhone *comes in two models;*
the iPhone 6s *and the* iPhone 6s Plus.
They are both sophisticated and highly
capable smartphones which are able to
make calls, send texts and multimedia
messages, browse the web, take and store
videos and still photos, play games and
keep you organized professionally and
personally.

A Very Smart Smartphone!

Apple's first generation iPhone was launched in June 2007. Because of the advance publicity, there was a feeding frenzy when launch day came, with customers queuing for many hours to get their hands on an iPhone.

There were several reasons for the excitement, including the Apple brand (stylish, functional and innovative). People already loved the iPod, so a cell phone with iPod capabilities and a wide screen had major appeal. The sheer simplicity of operation, using a touchscreen rather than a plethora of buttons, had widespread appeal.

So this was a cell phone unlike any other. In addition to the usual telephony capabilities, this phone could play music, videos, YouTube and more. It could be used as a diary with easy synchronization to Microsoft Outlook or Apple Calendar. It could handle email (including Exchange Server) more easily. Its SMS app made messaging a breeze. Its browser made browsing the web easier than with previous smartphones.

In addition, there were apps such as Weather, Stocks and Maps, amongst others. Despite criticisms from some parties regarding the poor camera (2 megapixels in the first and second generation iPhones) and lack of video, along with the inability for the user to add more apps, the first generation iPhone was a huge success.

The second generation iPhone was launched in July 2008 and brought with it 3G, a much faster data network connection. In June 2009 the 3GS ("S" stands for "speed") was launched. The new iPhone 3GS brought with it the ability to capture video, Voice Control, which enables users to control the iPhone 3GS using voice commands, and numerous other features.

The 4G iPhone was launched in June 2010 and brought with it many refinements such as dual cameras, camera flash, FaceTime, Siri (the voice controlled assistant), higher resolution Retina Display screen and many other improvements over the previous models. The 4GS was launched in Summer 2011, followed by the iPhone 5, iPhone 5c, 5s and 6/6 Plus in subsequent years.

The iPhone 6s was launched in September 2015 and comes in the standard iPhone 6s model and also the iPhone 6s Plus, which has a larger screen. Both models have retina HD screens: 4.7 inches for the iPhone 6s and 5.5 inches for the iPhone 6s Plus.

The iPhone 6s and iPhone 6s Plus both have similar storage options (they both come in 16GB, 64GB and 128GB models), a 12 megapixel iSight camera, and an A9 chip processor. The main difference between the two is the weight and the screen sizes.

Because the iPhone 6s and iPhone 6s Plus are generally the same, other than their size and weight, they will both be referred to as iPhone 6s, or just iPhone, unless required otherwise.

The New icon pictured above indicates a new or enhanced feature introduced with the iPhone 6s with iOS 9.

What Does It Do?

It would be easier to ask what it *doesn't* do! The iPhone, even as a basic cell phone before you start adding applications, has many functions – probably enough for most people, without then adding more apps of your own. But, since there are *thousands* of applications available for download, you can extend the functionality of the iPhone way beyond this. The iPhone is more like a small computer, as you can store files, email, connect to other desktop computers, view documents including Word and PDF files, play games, look up recipes, manage your time, as well as many other functions.

The iPhone is more like a computer than a standard cell phone.

Apps for work and play   Camera   On/Off button

Press and hold the On/Off button to turn on the iPhone, or access screen options for turning it off. Press it once to lock the iPhone and put it into Sleep mode, or to wake it up from Sleep mode.

Settings to customize your iPhone   App Store for more apps

In terms of color, you can get the iPhone 6s with a backing color of Silver, Gold, Space Gray or Rose Gold.

You cannot remove the iPhone battery. This has to be carried out by Apple.

If you intend to keep videos as well as music on your iPhone it may be wise to opt for the higher capacity iPhone.

iPhone 6s Specifications

Processor
Both of the iPhone 6s models come with an A9 processor, with 64-bit architecture.

Cameras
Both of the iPhone 6s models have a 12MP (megapixel) iSight camera for high quality photos and 4K video; and a 5MP front facing camera for photos and FaceTime video calls.

Cellular and wireless capabilities
The iPhone 6s is a Quad band phone which uses GSM and GPRS/EDGE.

There is also built-in Wi-Fi (802.11a/b/g/n/ac) and Bluetooth 4.2. The iPhone also includes Global Positioning System (GPS) software, making it easy to geotag (see page 32) your pictures and videos. The iPhone 6s also uses 3G and 4G networks where available. Check with your preferred carrier to see if they support 4G.

Battery
Unlike most cell phones, the user cannot take the battery out for replacement. The iPhone uses a built-in battery which is charged using a USB connection to the computer, or using the Lightning charger supplied by Apple.

What do you get from a full charge? (iPhone 6s or iPhone 6s Plus)
- Talk time: Up to 14 or 24 hours on 3G

- Standby time: Up to 10 days or 16 days

- Internet use: Up to 10 hours on 3G, up to 11 hours Wi-Fi; or 12 hours for both 3G and Wi-Fi

- Video playback: Up to 11 or 14 hours

- Audio playback: Up to 50 or 80hours

Internal storage
The iPhone uses internal flash drive storage. There is no SD or other card slot so the internal flash memory is all the storage you have – use it wisely!

Both iPhone 6s models are available with 16GB, 64GB or 128GB storage capacity.

What can I do with the storage space?

	16GB	64GB	128GB
Songs:	3,500	14,000	28,000
Videos:	20 hour	80 hours	160 hours
Photos:	20,000	50,000	100,000

Beware

The amount of storage space for songs, videos and photos can vary depending on the way the content has been created, particularly for videos and photos.

Sensors in the iPhone

There are four sensors in the iPhone: the Three-Axis Gyro, the Accelerometer, the Proximity Sensor and the Ambient Light Sensor.

The *Accelerometer* and *Three-Axis Gyro* enable the phone to detect rotation and position. This is important when switching from portrait to landscape viewing. The Accelerometer is also used in many of the iPhone game apps such as *Labyrinth* (below) which uses the Accelerometer to good effect – as you tilt the iPhone, the ball bearing moves across a virtual board.

The *Proximity Sensor* switches off the iPhone screen when you make a call – it senses that the phone is close to the ear, saving valuable power. The *Ambient Light Sensor* adjusts the iPhone screen to the ambient lighting, again saving energy if a bright screen is not required.

The iPhone Itself

Unlike some cell phones, the iPhone is unusual since it has very few physical buttons.

Buttons you need to know on the iPhone

- Sleep/Wake (On/Off)

- Ring/Silent

- Volume controls

- Home button

Hot tip

Press the Sleep/Wake (On/Off) button as soon as you have finished using the iPhone – this helps conserve battery power, by putting it into Sleep mode. Press the button again to wake up the iPhone. Pressing the Sleep/Wake (On/Off) button also manually locks the iPhone.

On/Off/Sleep/Wake up, on the right side of the body

Ring/Silent on the left side

Volume controls on the left side

Home button

On/Off/Sleep/Wake

Press and briefly hold this button if your iPhone is switched off. You will see the Apple logo and the loading screen will start up. You will then be taken to the Home screen, also known as the Homepage (see opposite page). If you wish to put your phone away, press the On/Off/Sleep/Wake button to put your phone to sleep.

Ring/Silent

You often want your phone on silent, during meetings for example. The Ring/Silent button can be toggled up and down. When you see the red line, this means the iPhone is on silent.

Pressing the Home button takes you back to the Home screen from any app you are using.

Home button

This does what the name suggests and brings you back to the Home screen from wherever you are. If you are browsing applications in another screen, pressing the Home button will bring you right back to the Home screen. If you are using an app, pressing Home returns you to the Home screen and the app stays open in the background. If you are on a phone call, pressing the Home button lets you access your email or other apps.

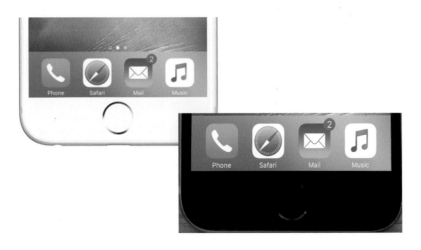

On the iPhone 6s the Home button can also be used as a fingerprint sensor for unlocking the phone with your unique fingerprint (see page 43).

Other Buttons on the iPhone

Volume controls

Volume is controlled using two separate buttons – a **+** and **–** button (increase and decrease volume respectively). You can easily adjust the volume of the audio output when you are listening to the Music app, or when you are making a phone call. If you cannot hear the caller very well, try increasing the volume.

There are no visual symbols on the volume buttons: the volume down button is below the volume up button.

Ring/silent

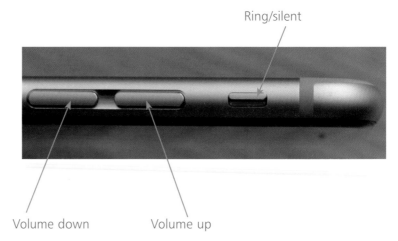

Volume down   Volume up

Nano SIM slot

The iPhone 6s uses a nano SIM (smaller than the micro SIM which is used in older iPhone models). Apple provides a SIM removal tool in the iPhone box.

Insert the SIM tool into this hole and push it firmly. The SIM card holder will pop out and you can remove it and insert a nano SIM card.

Lightning connector, speaker, microphone, and headset jack
These are located at the bottom of the iPhone.

Headset jack   Lightning connector

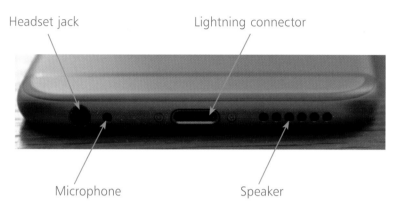

Microphone   Speaker

Back view of the iPhone 6s
This shows the location of the main iSight camera and the LED flash (flash is not available for the front-facing camera).

LED flash (and torch)

Rear microphone

iSight camera

The iSight camera can capture high quality photos at a resolution of 12 megapixels.

Setting up Your iPhone

Before you can do anything on your iPhone you will need to activate it.

Once you switch on the new iPhone 6s (press the On/Off button) you will be taken through a series of screens where you set up various options.

Even though the setup is carried out wirelessly, you can back up your iPhone by connecting it to iTunes on a Mac or PC, or backups can be done automatically through iCloud.

The setup screens include the following options (a lot of these can be skipped during the setup and accessed later from the **Settings** app):

- **Language**. Select the language you want to use.

- **Country**. Select your current country or region.

The selected language also determines the format of the keyboard, e.g. US English or UK English.

- **Wi-Fi network**. Select a Wi-Fi network to connect to the internet. If you are at home, this will be your own Wi-Fi network, if available. If you are at a Wi-Fi hotspot then this will appear on your network list.

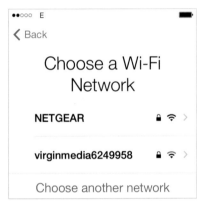

- **Location Services**. This determines whether your iPhone can use your geographical location for apps that use this type of information (such as Maps).

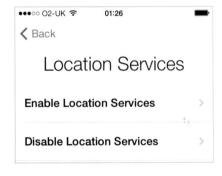

- **Set Up iPhone**. You can use this to set up your iPhone from scratch, or restore it from a backup that has been created via iCloud or on iTunes on a Mac computer.

- **Apple ID**. You can register with this to be able to access a range of Apple facilities, such as iCloud, purchase items on iTunes or the App Store, FaceTime, Messages and iBooks. You can also create an Apple ID whenever you first access one of the relevant apps.

An Apple ID can also be created from the Apple website at: **appleid.apple.com**

- **iCloud**. This is Apple's online service for sharing and backing up content. See pages 52-64 for details.

- **Find My iPhone**. This is a service that can be activated so that you can locate your iPhone if it is lost or stolen. This is done via the online iCloud site at **www.icloud.com**

- **Touch ID**. This can be used on the iPhone 6s to create a fingerprint ID that can be used to unlock the phone.

- **Create a Passcode**. This can be used to create a four-digit code for unlocking the phone. This step can be skipped if required.

Touch ID can also be used to make payments with Apple Pay, once it is set up. For more details, see pages 44-47.

- **Siri**. This is the voice assistant that can be used to find things on your iPhone and on the web.

- **Diagnostic information**. This enables information about your iPhone to be sent to Apple.

- **Display Zoom**. This can be used to increase the size of the display so that the icons are larger.

- **Get Started**. Once the setup process has been completed you can start using your iPhone.

17

Beware

As you download more apps from the App Store these will be placed on subsequent Home screens, as each one gets filled up.

Beware

The default Battery indicator is fairly basic. For a more accurate guide, turn on the battery percentage on the status bar at the top of the screen. To do this, open **Settings > Battery** and turn **Battery Percentage** to **On**.

The Home Screen

What's on the Home screen?

When you turn the iPhone on you will see some icons which are fixed, such as the top bar with the time and battery charge indicator, as well as the Dock at the bottom which holds four apps. By default, your iPhone will have Phone, Safari, Mail and Music on the bottom Dock. You can move these off the Dock if you want, but Apple puts these here because they are deemed to be the most commonly-used apps, and having them on the Dock makes them easy to find.

Just above the Dock you will see two dots. The dots represent each of your screens – the more apps you install, the more screens you will need to accommodate them (you are allowed 11 in all). The illustration here shows an iPhone with two screens, and the Home screen is the one we are viewing. If you flicked to the next screen, the second dot would be white and the first one would be gray. In effect, these are meant to let you know where you are at any time.

Signal strength, network and Wi-Fi   Time   Battery

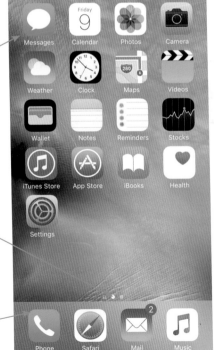

Default apps (which can be moved around but not deleted)

Dots representing the number of screens. Tap on a dot to move to that screen, or swipe left and right to move between screens

The Dock, where apps can be placed, which appears on all screens

Default Applications

The iPhone comes with applications that are part of the operating system. The core set here cannot be deleted.

 Messages

 Notes

 Calendar

 Photos

 Calculator

 Clock

 Camera

 iBooks

 Maps

 Podcasts

 Phone

 Weather

 Stocks

 Wallet

 Mail

 Voice Memos

 Safari

 Game Center

 Music

 Videos

 News

 Reminders

 Contacts

 Health

You cannot delete any of the pre-installed apps – only the ones you add yourself.

As well as those shown, Settings, App Store and iTunes Store are default apps, and they link to specific settings or services.

Other useful apps, such as Trailers, iMovie, GarageBand, Pages, Numbers and Keynote can be downloaded from the App Store.

The iPhone Dock

By default, there are four apps on the Dock at the bottom of the screen. These are the four that Apple thinks you will use most frequently:

- **Phone**, for calls
- **Safari**, for web browsing
- **Mail**, for email
- **Music**, for listening to music

Hot tip

Just above the Dock is a line of small white dots. These indicate how many screens of content there are on the iPhone. Tap on one of the dots to go to that screen.

You can rearrange the order in which the Dock apps appear:

1 Tap and hold on one of the Dock apps until it starts to jiggle

2 Drag the app into its new position

3 Click once on the **Home** button to return from edit mode

Adding and removing Dock apps

You can also remove apps from the Dock and add new ones:

1 To remove an app from the Dock, tap and hold it and drag it onto the main screen area

2 To add an app to the Dock, tap and hold it and drag it onto the Dock

Don't forget

If items are removed from the Dock they are still available in the same way from the main screen.

21

3 The number of items that can be added to the Dock is restricted to a maximum of four, as the icons do not resize

4 Click once on the **Home** button to return from edit mode

About iOS 9

iOS 9 is the latest version of the operating system for Apple's mobile devices including the iPhone, the iPad and the iPod Touch. It is an incremental update from the previous version, iOS 8, with some new features and updates, rather than a complete visual and technical overhaul of the iOS.

Linking it all up

One of the features of iOS 8, which is continued in iOS 9, is the way it links up with other Apple devices, whether it is something like an iPad also using iOS 9, or an Apple desktop or laptop computer running the OS X El Capitan operating system. This works with apps such as Mail and Photos, so you can start an email on one device and finish it on another, or take a photo on one device and have it available on all other compatible Apple devices. Most of this is done through iCloud, and once it is set up it takes care of most of these tasks automatically. (See Chapter Two for details about setting up and using iCloud.)

Don't forget

To check the version of the iOS, look in **Settings > General > Software Update**.

3D Touch and improved apps

Some of the updates to the iPhone 6s with iOS 9 are an evolution of what came before: an improved camera with a 12 megapixel resolution; the widening of availability for the Apple Pay contactless payment system; the expansion of the Music app to include Apple Music, which offers access to the entire iTunes Music library (subscription required after initial three-month free trial); enhancements to the Notes app so that notes can be created by scribbling on the screen and photos and lists added. In addition, there is also a 3D Touch function where different options can be viewed within apps, depending on how hard you press on the screen, either in compatible apps or those on the Home screen.

iOS 9 is an operating system that is stylish and versatile on the iPhone, and it also plays an important role in computing: linking desktop and mobile devices so that users can spend more time doing the things that matter to them, safe in the knowledge that their content will be backed up and available across multiple devices.

The Touch Screen Display

The iPhone uses a touch-sensitive screen for input, using gestures and a virtual keyboard. The screen is 4.7 or 5.5 inches (diagonal) and has a resolution of 1136 x 750-pixel resolution at 326 PPI (Pixels Per Inch), or 1920 x 1080 at 401 PPI. Apple has called this the *Retina Display* because the resolution is so high. This results in great clarity when viewing the browser or watching movies on the iPhone.

Touch screen features

The screen is able to detect touch from skin, using these gestures:

Tapping

Tapping with one finger is used for lots of apps. It's a bit like clicking with the mouse. You can tap apps to open them, to open hyperlinks, to select photo albums which then open, to enter text using the keyboard, and many other tasks.

Sliding

You can use the slide action to answer phone calls, shut down the iPhone and unlock the Lock screen, as well as scrolling web pages, moving to the next Home screen and moving between photos.

Dragging

This is used to move documents that occupy more than a screen's worth across the screen. Maps use this feature, as do web pages. Place your finger on the screen, keep it there and move the image to where you want it.

Pinching and spreading

To zoom in on a photo, web page or map, swipe outwards with thumb and forefinger. Pinch inwards to zoom back out.

Minimizing the screen

One feature of the iPhone 6s is to make everything easily within reach. This can be done by minimizing the screen to enable you to comfortably access it when holding the iPhone with one hand. To do this, double-tap gently on the Home button.

The iPhone 6s has a 4.7 inch screen and the iPhone 6s Plus has the larger, 5.5 inch screen.

Although the iPhone has a fingerprint-resistant coating it still gets grubby. A number of companies make screen protectors, and you can also protect the other parts of the iPhone from scratching by using a protective case.

Flicking

If you are faced with a long list, e.g. in Contacts, you can flick the list up or down by placing your finger at the bottom or top of the screen, keeping your finger on the screen, then flicking your finger downwards or upwards and the list will fly up or down.

Shake the iPhone

After entering text or copying and pasting, to undo what you have done, shake the iPhone and select Undo. Shake again to select Redo.

Portrait or landscape mode

The iPhone is generally viewed in a portrait mode, but for many tasks it is easier to turn the iPhone and work in landscape mode. If you're in Mail, or using Safari, the coverage will be larger. More importantly, the keys of the virtual keyboard become larger making it easier to type accurately.

Entering text

The iPhone has predictive text, but this is unlike any you may have used before. The accuracy is astonishing. As you type, the iPhone will make suggestions before you complete a word. If you agree with the suggested word, tap the spacebar. If you disagree, tap the small "x" next to the word.

You can shake your iPhone to skip audio tracks, undo and redo text, and more.

To accept a spelling suggestion, tap the spacebar. Reject the suggestion by clicking the "x". Over time, your iPhone will learn new words.

Double-tap the spacebar to insert a period (full stop) followed by a space, ready for the next sentence to begin.

Accept the capitalized word by tapping the spacebar

Accept the apostrophe by tapping the spacebar

App Switcher Window

The iPhone can run several apps at once and these can be managed by the App Switcher window. This performs a number of useful functions:

- It shows open apps.

- It enables you to move between open apps and access different ones, e.g. make them the active app.

- It enables apps to be closed (see next page).

Accessing the App Switcher
The App Switcher option can be accessed from any screen on your iPhone, as follows:

1 Double-click on the **Home** button

2 The currently-open apps are displayed, with their icons above them. The most recently-used apps are shown first

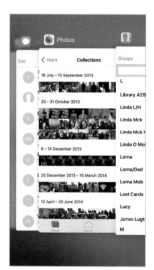

3 Swipe left and right to view the open apps. Tap on one to access it in full-screen size, e.g. make it the active app

Closing Items

The iPhone deals with open apps very efficiently. They do not interact with other apps, unless required, which increases security and also means that they can be open in the background, without using up a significant amount of processing power, in a state of semi-hibernation until they are needed. Because of this, it is not essential to close apps when you move to something else. However, you may want to close apps if you feel you have too many open or if one stops working. To do this:

1 Access the App Switcher window. The currently-open apps are displayed

2 Press and hold on an app and swipe it to the top of the screen to close it. This does not remove it from the iPhone and it can be opened again in the usual way

When you switch from one app to another, the first one stays open in the background. You can go back to it by accessing it from the App Switcher window or the Home screen.

Don't forget

27

3 The app is removed from its position in the App Switcher window

In the Control Center

The Control Center is a panel containing some of the most commonly used options within the **Settings** app. It can be accessed with one swipe and is an excellent function for when you do not want to have to go into Settings.

Accessing the Control Center

The Control Center can be accessed from any screen within iOS 9 and it can also be accessed from the Lock screen:

1 Tap on the **Settings** app

2 Tap on the **Control Center** tab and drag the **Access on Lock Screen** and **Access Within Apps** buttons On or Off to specify if the Control Center can be accessed from here (if both are Off, it can still be accessed from any Home screen)

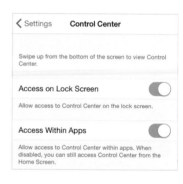

3 Swipe up from the bottom of any screen to access the Control Center panel

4 Tap on this button to hide the Control Center panel, or tap anywhere on the background screen

5 Use this slider to control the screen brightness

Beware

The Control Center cannot be disabled from being accessed from the Home screen.

Control Center controls

The items that can be used in the Control Center are:

1 Use these controls for any music or video that is playing. Use the buttons to Pause/Play a track, go to the beginning or end and adjust the volume

2 Tap on this button to turn **Airplane mode** On or Off

3 Tap on this button to turn **Wi-Fi** On or Off

4 Tap on this button to turn **Bluetooth** On or Off

5 Tap on this button to turn **Do Not Disturb mode** On or Off

6 Tap on this button to **Lock** or **Unlock** screen rotation. If it is locked, the screen will not change when you change the orientation of your iPhone

7 Tap on this button to activate the iPhone's **Torch**

8 Tap on this button to access a **Clock**, including a stopwatch

9 Tap on this button to open the **Calculator** app

10 Tap on this button to open the **Camera** app

Don't forget

When Airplane mode is activated, the network and wireless connectivity on the iPhone is disabled. However, it can still be used for functions such as playing music or reading books.

Hot tip

The Torch function is very effective, particularly over short distances.

Don't forget

There is also an AirDrop link which is covered on page 109.

29

The Virtual Keyboard

The keys are small but when you touch them they become larger, which increases accuracy. The letter "T" below has been pressed and has become much larger.

The iPhone has done away with virtually all buttons and provides a software-based QWERTY keyboard. The keyboard becomes visible automatically when needed. When you press on a key it expands so that you can see it more clearly.

There are all the usual features of a computer keyboard, including spacebar, delete key , shift , numbers and symbols

To correct a word, touch the word you want to correct and hold your finger on the word. You will see a magnifying glass. Move your finger to where you want the insertion point (|) to be, stop there and delete any wrong letters.

Some keys such as Currency and URL endings can be accessed by holding down the key. A pop-up will show the options.

The keyboard has automatic spellcheck and correction of misspelled words. It has a dynamic dictionary which learns new words as you type. Some keys have multiple options if you hold them down, e.g. hold down the $ key and you'll see the other characters.

Where's Caps Lock?

It is frustrating hitting the Caps key for every letter if you want to type a complete word in upper case. But you can activate Caps Lock easily:

1 Go to **Settings > General**

2 Select **Keyboard**

3 Make sure the **Enable Caps Lock** slider is set to **On**

4 While you are there, make sure the other settings are on, for example **"." Shortcut** – this helps you add a period (full stop) by tapping the spacebar twice

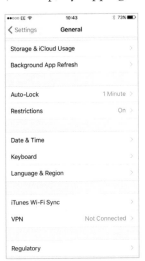
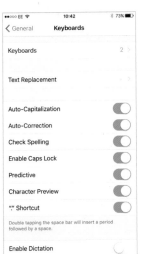

Other settings for the keyboard

- **Auto-Correction** suggests the correct word. If it annoys you, switch it off.

- **Auto-Capitalization** is great for putting capitals in names.

- Whilst the **"." Shortcut** types a period every time you hit the spacebar twice and saves time when typing long emails, if you prefer not to use this, you can switch it off. Here's another neat trick – you can also insert a period by tapping the spacebar with two fingers simultaneously.

Hot tip

It's a good idea to activate Caps Lock. To use, just tap Shift twice – the shift button should have a black, upwards pointing arrow on it with a black bar underneath it if you have activated it properly in the Settings.

Hot tip

If you do not like the default iPhone keyboard, you can download third-party ones from the App Store. Some to look at include SwiftKey, Swype and KuaiBoard.

Camera

The iPhone 6s has a main (iSight) camera on the back of the phone, and a second camera on the front. The main camera is 12 megapixels (MP), and can shoot high resolution stills and 4K video (3840 by 2160 at 30 frames per second), or HD video at 1080p up to 60 frames per second. The main camera also has a True Tone flash. The front VGA camera is used for FaceTime calls, and can take photos and videos at 5 MP (photos) and HD video (720p).

Both photos and videos can be geotagged, so you can see where in the world you were, when the photo or video was shot.

Geotagging helps you determine where the photo was taken, but you need to switch it on in **Settings > Privacy > Location Services > Camera > Allow Location > While Using the App**.

Tap on this button so that it turns yellow, to activate Live Photos. This is a short animated clip that is captured in normal photo mode by tapping on the button in Step 2. It creates a short movie file that can be played in the Photos app by pressing and holding on it, or you can send it to someone as a video. Tap on the button again to deactivate Live Photos.

1 Swipe left and right here to move between standard photo mode, square mode, panorama, video, slow-mo and time-lapse

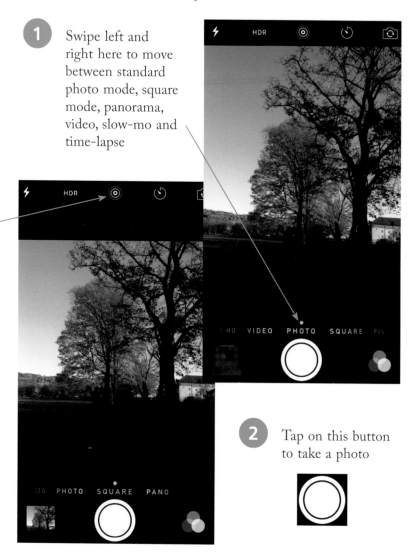

2 Tap on this button to take a photo

3 Tap on this button to toggle between the front- and back-facing cameras

Don't forget

The iPhone iSight camera has an improved autofocus system, improved face detection and image stabilization for improved clarity.

4 Tap on this button to select a filter effect to add to the photo you are going to take

Don't forget

The iPhone iSight camera can capture high quality video at 4K standard, which records at 3840 x 2160 pixels at 30 frames per second (fps).

Shooting video

Select the Video option as shown in Step 1 and you will see a Record button (red circle). Press to record video then press again to stop recording.

00:00:05

Don't forget

See pages 110-118 for how to view and edit photos and videos you have taken.

Searching with Spotlight

If you want to find things on your iPhone, there is a built-in search engine: Spotlight. This can search over numerous items on your iPhone, and these can be selected within Settings.

Spotlight settings

Within the Settings app you can select which items the Spotlight search operates over. To do this:

1 Tap on the **Settings** app

2 Tap on **General** tab

3 Tap on the **Spotlight Search** link

4 Tap on an item to exclude it from the Spotlight search. Items with a tick will be included

Accessing Spotlight

The Spotlight Search box can be accessed from any screen by pressing and swiping downwards on any free area of the Home screen. This also activates the keyboard. Enter the search keywords into the Search box at the top of the window. Swipe up the page to view the range of results (the keyboard disappears when you swipe up the page).

Searching with Siri

Siri is the iPhone digital voice assistant that provides answers to a variety of questions by looking at your iPhone and also web services. Initially, Siri can be set up within the **Settings** app:

1 In the **General** section, tap on the **Siri** link

Siri	>

2 Drag the **Siri** button to **On** to activate the Siri functionality. Tap on the links to select a language, set voice feedback and allow access to your details

Questioning Siri

Once you have set up Siri, you can start putting it to work with your queries. To do this:

1 Hold down the **Home** button until the Siri window appears

2 Ask a question such as, **Show me my calendar, Siri**

3 The results are displayed by Siri. Tap on an item to view its details. Tap on the microphone button to ask another question of Siri

Hot tip

You can ask Siri questions relating to the apps on your iPhone and also general questions, such as weather conditions around the world, or sports results. The results will be displayed by Siri, or, if it does not know the answer, a web or Wikipedia link will be displayed instead.

Headphones

Apple supplies headphones that look a bit like iPod headphones, but there is a major difference: the iPhone headphones have a control on the right earpiece cable. This control houses the microphone needed for phone conversations when the headphones are plugged in. The control also allows the audio volume to be adjusted, to make it louder or quieter.

By clicking the control, audio will pause. Two clicks in quick succession will skip to the next track.

The iPhone headphones are highly sophisticated and can be used to make calls, and also divert callers to voicemail.

The iPhone supports a number of audio and video formats. The iPhone supports audio formats including AAC, Protected AAC, MP3, MP3 VBR, Audible (formats 2, 3, and 4), Apple Lossless, AIFF and WAV. In terms of video, the iPhone supports formats including 4k, MPEG-4, Motion JPEG and .mov file formats.

Press here ONCE to pause audio or answer call (press again at end of call)

To decline call press and hold for ~2 seconds

To switch to incoming or on-hold call, press once

Press here TWICE to skip to next track

To use Voice Control, press and hold

(this tiny control unit also contains the microphone!)

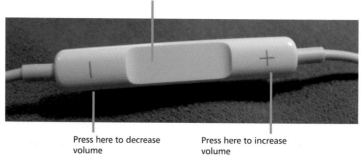

Press here to decrease volume

Press here to increase volume

Uses for the headphones – this is pretty obvious but consider

- Listening to music, podcasts, audio books

- Listening to the radio

- Watching movies

- Making phone calls

- Dictating Voice Memos

- Giving Voice commands to your iPhone

Customizing the iPhone

Applications

The iPhone comes with many apps pre-installed by Apple. These can be moved around, or even placed on a different screen, but you cannot delete them from the iPhone. These apps are the core features of the iPhone.

The App Store has thousands of apps which we will look at later. Many are free while others are available for purchase. With so many apps available for download, the chances are that there will be an app for most things you might want to do.

Ringtones

Apple has supplied several, but people will always want to have their own unique ringtone. You can buy these from the App Store or make your own using iTunes or GarageBand. You can assign a specific ringtone to someone in your Contacts list so you know it's them calling when the phone rings.

Backgrounds and wallpapers

Again, there are several to choose from but you can make your own (use one of your photos) or you can download from third-party suppliers. Try browsing the internet for wallpapers or use a specific app.

Accessorizing the iPhone

You can use a screen protector to prevent scratches on the screen. There are also many iPhone cases available. These are mainly plastic, but leather cases are available as well. Placing your iPhone in a case or cover helps prevent marks or scratches on the phone.

Headphones

If you want to use headphones other than those provided by Apple, that's fine. You may get better sound from your music but you will not have the inbuilt microphone, which is very useful when you make a phone call.

USB to Lightning charger cable

With extensive use, the iPhone battery may not last the whole day so you will probably need to carry around a spare charging cable. The USB to Lightning cable means you can plug it in to your PC or Mac at work and charge your iPhone during the day.

GarageBand is Apple's music-making app and it can be downloaded from the App Store.

Bluetooth drains power on your iPhone. Try to switch it off if you don't need it.

User Settings

There are many settings you can adjust in order to set the iPhone up to work the way you want. These are accessed from the **Settings** app.

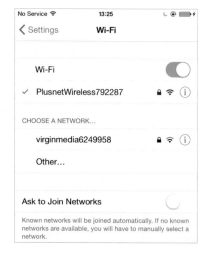

As well as the settings already on the iPhone, many apps will have panels for their settings. If an app is not working the way you want, have a look under the Settings Control Panel and scroll to the bottom to see if your app has installed a settings panel.

The **Wi-Fi** Settings are grouped together with those for **Airplane Mode**, **Bluetooth**, **Cellular** and **Carrier**. Bluetooth can be used to scan for other compatible devices, which then have to be paired with the iPhone so that they can share content wirelessly.

Wi-Fi

Keep this off if you want to conserve power. Switching it on will let you join wireless networks if they are open or if you have the password.

Notifications

This is where you can set what items appear in the Notification Center, which is accessed by swiping down from the top of the screen.

Control Center

This is a set of shortcuts for regularly used items. See pages 28-29 for details.

Do Not Disturb

Use this to specify times when you do not receive alerts or FaceTime video calls.

If a Settings option has an On/Off button next to it, this can be changed by swiping the button to either the left or right. Green indicates that the option is **On**.

General

This contains the largest range of settings, which can be used to check the software version on your iPhone, search settings, accessibility, storage, date and time, keyboard settings and resetting your iPhone.

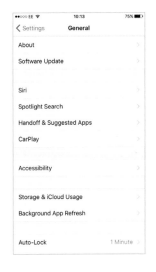

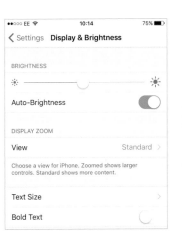

Display & Brightness

This can be used for adjusting the screen brightness, the display viewing size and using larger text sizes, or bold text.

The screen brightness can also be adjusted from the Control Center.

Wallpaper

Wallpaper is what you see when you press the Home button, and when the iPhone is locked. Use your own images or download from third party suppliers.

...cont'd

Sounds

You can place the phone on vibrate or have the ringtone on. You can assign different tones for different contacts.

Touch ID & Passcode

This can be used to set up fingerprint security for unlocking your iPhone and also a numerical passcode (see page 43 for more details).

Battery

This can be used to put the iPhone into low power mode to save power, and view battery usage for specific apps.

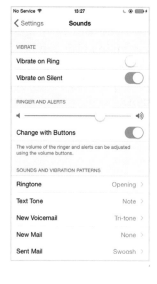

Hot tip

You can assign specific ringtones to selected contacts.

Privacy

This contains a number of privacy options, including activating **Location Services**, so that apps such as Maps and Siri can use your location, using GPS. Location Services also has to be turned On if you want to use the **Find My iPhone** feature.

Hot tip

One of the iCloud functions is the iCloud Keychain (**Settings > iCloud > Keychain**). If this is enabled, it can keep all of your passwords and credit card information up-to-date across multiple devices and remember them when you use them on websites. The information is encrypted and controlled through your Apple ID.

iCloud

This is where you can specify the items that are shared with the online iCloud service. This includes On/Off options for apps such as Notes and Calendars, and additional options for the Photos app.

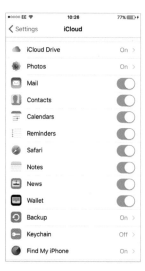

iTunes & App Stores

This can be used to specify settings for
the online iTunes and App Store, such
as enabling automatic downloads when
there are updates to your existing apps or
music.

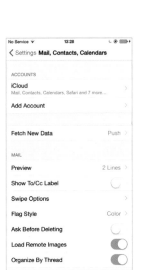

Mail, Contacts, Calendars

Use this for setting up new email
accounts and also specifying settings
for your existing accounts.

Apps' Settings

A lot of apps have their own settings,
including the pre-installed ones. Tap
on an app's name in the Settings app
to view its own specific settings. It
is worth checking Settings after you
install an app to see if it has installed a
settings file, since it may contain useful
features to help you set it up exactly
the way you want.

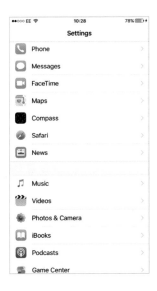

Using the Lock Screen

To save power, it is possible to set your iPhone screen to auto-lock. This is the equivalent of the sleep option on a traditional computer. To do this:

1 Tap on the **Settings** app

Don't forget

You can also lock the iPhone using the **On/Off** button on the right-hand side of the phone. Press once to lock, and press again to display the Lock screen, as shown in Step 5.

2 Tap on the **General** tab

 General

3 Tap on the **Auto-Lock** link

Auto-Lock   1 Minute >

4 Tap on the time of non-use after which you wish the screen to be locked

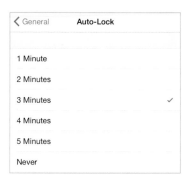

5 Once the screen is locked, swipe here to the right to unlock the screen

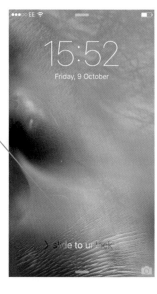

Touch ID

Fingerprint sensor

The iPhone 6s has a fingerprint sensor that can be used to unlock your iPhone. This is done by pressing your thumb or finger on the sensor to create a unique fingerprint code. To set this up:

1 Select **Settings > Touch ID & Passcode**

2 A passcode is required before Touch ID can be activated. Tap on the **Turn Passcode On** link

3 Enter a four-digit passcode

4 Tap on the **Add a Fingerprint** link. This presents a screen for creating your Touch ID. Place your finger on the Home button several times until the Touch ID is created. Use this to unlock your iPhone at the Lock screen

The Touch ID function can also be used with Apple's contactless payment system, Apple Pay, see pages 44-47.

The fingerprint sensor is very effective, although it may take a bit of practice until you can get the right position for your finger to unlock the iPhone, first time, every time.

About Apple Pay

Apple Pay is Apple's service for mobile, contactless payment. It can be used by adding credit, debit and store cards to your iPhone 6s, via the Wallet app, and then paying for items by using your Touch ID fingerprint as authorization for payment. Credit, debit and store cards have to be issued by banks or retailers who support Apple Pay, but there are an increasing number that do so, with more joining on a regular basis. Outlets also have to support Apple Pay but this too is increasing and, given the success of the iPhone, is likely to grow at a steady rate.

Setting up Apple Pay

To use Apple Pay you have to add your cards to your iPhone 6s:

1 Tap once on the **Wallet** app

2 Tap once on the **Add Credit or Debit Card** link or tap once on this button

 Pay

Pay with Touch ID using Apple Pay. Make purchases in stores and in apps without swiping your card or entering your card and shipping details.

Add Credit or Debit Card

3 Tap once on the **Next** button

Cancel   Next

Don't forget

At the time of printing, Apple Pay is only available in the US, UK, Canada and Australia. In the UK there is a limit of £30 for in-store purchases, but there is no such limit in the US, Canada or Australia.

Hot tip

Cards can also be added to the Wallet at any time from **Settings > Wallet & Apple Pay > Add Credit or Debit Card**.

Don't forget

If your bank does not yet support Apple Pay then you will not be able to add your credit or debit card details into the Wallet app.

4 The card details can be added to the Wallet by taking a photo of the card. Place the card on a flat surface and position it within the white box. The card number is then added automatically. Alternatively, tap once on the **Enter Card Details Manually** link

Beware

Obtaining your card number using the camera is not always completely accurate. Take the photo in good light and always check the number afterwards and amend it if necessary.

5 Tap once on the **Next** button to verify your card details (ensure the name is exactly the same as it appears on the card)

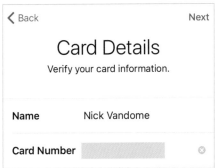

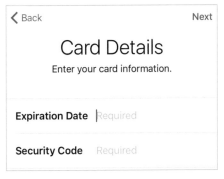
Don't forget

During the setup process you will also have to **Agree** to the Apple Pay Terms and Conditions.

6 Add any additional details for the card (such as expiration date and the security code) and tap once on the **Next** button. (If the card has already been registered for use on iTunes, the details will be shown here.)

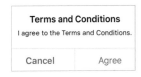

...cont'd

Although no form of contactless payment is 100% secure, Apple Pay does offer some security safeguards. One is that no card information is passed between the retailer and the user: the transaction is done by sending an encrypted token that is used to authorize the payment. Also, the use of the Touch ID fingerprint ensures another step of authorization that is not available with all other forms of contactless payment.

You will be sent a text message, or will receive a phone call, stating the verification code, if selected.

Numerous cards can be added within the Wallet app.

7 Before you can use Apple Pay, your bank or store card issuer has to verify your card. This can be done either by a text message or a phone call. Select the preferred method and tap once on the **Next** button

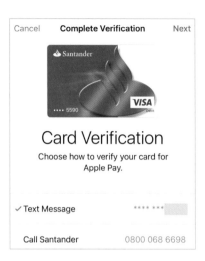

8 If you selected to verify your card with a text message in Step 7, you will be sent a code to verify your card. Enter this, and tap once on the **Next** button. Once this has been done, the card will be activated. Tap once on the **Done** button on the Card Activated screen

9 Details of the card that has been added to the Wallet are displayed. This will be visible when you open the Wallet app, ready for use with Apple Pay

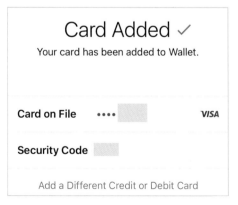

Using Apple Pay

Once credit, debit and store cards have been added to the Wallet app and authorized by the issuer, they can be used with Apple Pay in participating outlets. To do this:

1 When you go to pay for an item, open the **Wallet** app and tap once on the card you want to use. Press the **Home** button to authorize the payment with Touch ID using your unique fingerprint

Pay with Touch ID

Hot tip

Cards for Apple Pay can be accessed directly from the Lock screen, if this has been set up: **Settings > Wallet & Apple Pay** and turn On **Double-Click Home Button** under **Allow Access When Locked**.

2 Hold your iPhone 6s up to the contactless payment card reader. (Retailers must have a contactless card reader in order for Apple Pay to be used.) The payment should be processed

Hold Near Reader to Pay

Don't forget

Apple Pay can also be used on some online sites, in which case the Apple Pay logo will be displayed.

3 To view your payments, tap once on the Wallet app and select a card. The latest transaction is displayed, but not specific items that you have bought. This information is only visible to you and is not shared with Apple. Select **Settings > Wallet & Apple Pay** to view a longer list of transactions

LAST TRANSACTION
Co-Op Group Food   £4.78
1 Hour Ago - Perth, Scotland

Don't forget

The Wallet app can also be used to scan items such as boarding passes and cinema tickets, and then used from the Lock screen. However, this can only be done with participating organizations.

Using 3D Touch

One of the innovations on the iPhone 6s with iOS 9 is 3D Touch. This can be used to activate different options for certain apps, depending on the strength with which you press on an item. For instance, a single press, or tap, can be used to open an app. However, if you press harder on the app then different options appear. This can be used for Quick Actions and Peek and Pop.

Quick Actions

These are some of the Quick Actions that can be accessed with 3D Touch:

1. Press deeper into the **Camera** app to access options for taking a selfie or recording a video, a slo-mo shot or a regular photo

2. Press deeper into the **Messages** app to access options for sending a text message to recent contacts or create a new message

3. Press deeper into the **Mail** app to access options for accessing your Inbox, adding a VIP, searching for an email or creating a new email

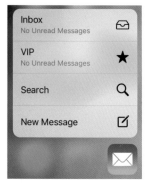

Peek and Pop

3D Touch can also be used to view items within apps, with a single press. This is known as Peek and Pop. To use this, with the Mail app:

1 Press on an email in your Inbox to peek at it, i.e. view it with the other items blurred out

2 Press deeper on the email to pop it open, i.e. view it in preview mode, rather than opening it fully. (Swipe up on the preview screen to access a menu for options for the email, e.g. Reply etc.)

3 Press deeper again on the email to open it fully in the Mail app and access its full functionality

Other apps that offer Quick Actions include: Notes, Safari, Music, Maps and Wallet.

Other apps that offer Peek and Pop include: Safari, Maps, Camera and Photos. Items for Safari and Maps can be peeked at and accessed from within an email, e.g. if there is a website link in an email, press it once to view a preview of the web page, and press deeper to open it in Safari. Photos can be peeked at from the Camera app by pressing on a thumbnail image and then pressing deeper to open it.

Data Roaming

Most of us travel abroad for business or pleasure. We like to take our cell phones to keep in touch with friends, family and the office. Call charges are much higher from overseas, and if you want to receive data (email, browse the web, and other activities) you will need to switch on Data Roaming.

Switch on Data Roaming

1 Go to **Settings > Cellular** (or **Mobile**)

2 Switch **Data Roaming** On if required

3 Switch Off when not needed

But beware – the cost of receiving data is very high and will be added to your phone bill. Your data package with your network supplier (e.g. AT&T, O2 etc.) will not cover the cost of downloading data using foreign networks!

Data Roaming allows you to receive data when away from your home country, but it can be very expensive.

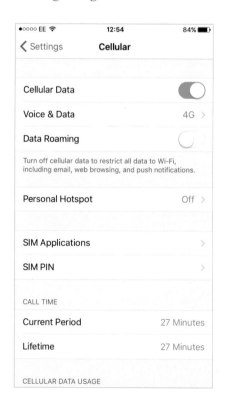

2 iPhone 6s and iCloud

iCloud is Apple's *online storage and backup service. This chapter shows how to set up an iCloud account and use it to save your content and make it available on any other iCloud-enabled devices you have. It also covers sharing your photos, music, books and apps with family members, using the Family Sharing feature.*

iCloud and an Apple ID

Apple iCloud

iCloud allows you to use the cloud to back up and sync your data (calendars, contacts, mail, Safari bookmarks, and notes) wirelessly.

Once you are registered and set up, any entries or deletions to Calendars and other apps are reflected in all devices using iCloud.

An Apple ID is required for using iCloud, and this can be obtained online at **https://appleid.apple.com/** or you can create an Apple ID when you first access an app on your iPhone that requires this for use. It is free to create an Apple ID and requires a username and password. Once you have created an Apple ID you can then use the full range of iCloud services.

Start using iCloud on the iPhone and computers

Don't forget

The iPhone apps that require an Apple ID to access their full functionality include: iTunes Store, App Store, Messages, iBooks, Game Center and FaceTime.

52

1 On your iPhone, open **Settings > iCloud** and select the items you want to be used by iCloud. All of the selected items will have their data saved to iCloud so that it is backed up. You will also be able to access these items from other iCloud-enabled devices, such as a computer (see below)

Don't forget

Using iCloud removes the need to sync items such as contacts, calendars, notes and photos on other iCloud-enabled devices that you have, such as tablets and computers: iCloud does it all automatically.

2 On your computer, open the iCloud System Preferences (Mac) or Control Panel (PC)

3 Log into your iCloud account with your Apple ID (you only need to do this once – it will remember your details)

4 Check **On** the items that you want to use with iCloud

Using iCloud online

Once you have created an Apple ID you will automatically have an iCloud account. This can be used to sync your data from your iPhone and you can also access your content online from the iCloud website at **www.icloud.com**

1 Enter your Apple ID details

2 Click on the **iCloud** button from any section to go to other areas

3 The full range of iCloud apps is displayed, including those for Pages, Numbers and Keynote

Hot tip

iCloud lets you sync emails, contacts, calendars and other items wirelessly (no need to physically plug the iPhone into the computer).

About the iCloud Drive

One of the options in the iCloud section is for the iCloud Drive. This can be used to store documents so that you can use them on any other Apple devices that you have, such as an iPhone or a MacBook. To set up iCloud Drive:

The apps that can be used with iCloud Drive are generally Apple's own apps, such as Pages, Numbers and Keynote for productivity. However, other app developers are also making more apps that are compatible with iCloud Drive. These will be displayed in the area in Step 3.

1 In the iCloud section of the Settings app, tap on the **iCloud Drive** button

2 Tap on the **iCloud Drive** button so that it is **On**

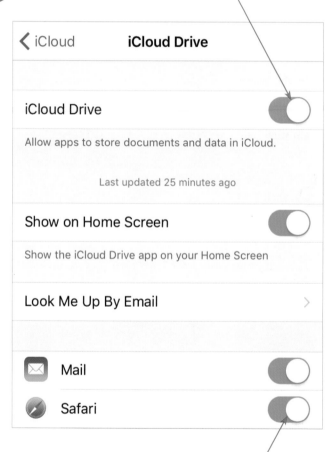

3 Once iCloud Drive has been activated, tap on any listed apps so that they can use iCloud Drive

4 When you are using an app that has iCloud Drive capabilities it may ask you to turn on iCloud Drive for that specific app, if it has not already been done. Tap on the **OK** button and open the Settings app

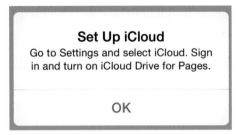

5 In the Settings app, open the settings for the specific app (in this case, Pages) and drag the **Use iCloud** button to **On**. Any document created or edited by this app will automatically be stored in the iCloud Drive

6 The documents in the app on your iPhone can be viewed on your other Apple devices if you have iCloud turned on and iCloud Drive activated. For iOS 9 devices they can be viewed from the Documents section of the compatible apps (such as Pages, Numbers and Keynote); for OS X Yosemite (or later) devices they can be viewed in the iCloud Drive section in the Finder

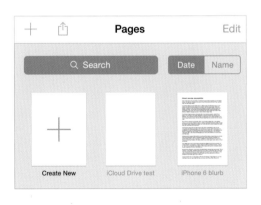

Using iCloud Drive Online

Files that have been saved to your iCloud Drive on your iPhone can also be accessed on any other Apple devices you have, such as an iPhone or a MacBook. They can also be accessed from your online iCloud account at **www.icloud.com**, from any internet-enabled computer. To do this:

1 Log in to your iCloud account and click on the iCloud Drive button on the Homepage

2 Your iCloud Drive folders are displayed. Content created within the relevant apps on your iPhone will automatically be stored in the appropriate folders, i.e. Pages documents in the Pages folder, etc.

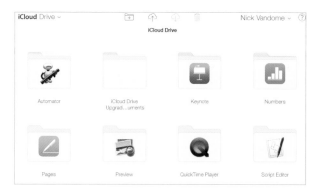

3 Click on a folder to view its contents. You can also edit documents or create new ones with the online iCloud. These changes will appear on your iPhone when the relevant apps are opened

Don't forget

If you make changes to an iCloud Drive document on your iPhone, the changes will be visible when you open the document on another iCloud-enabled device e.g. an iPad, with the same app as used to create the document.

Continuity and Handoff

One of the main themes of iOS 9 and the iPhone 6s is to make all of your content available on all of your Apple devices. This is known as Continuity and Handoff: when you create something on one device you can then pick it up and finish it on another device. This is done through iCloud. To do this:

1 Ensure the app has iCloud turned on

2 Create the content on the app on your iPhone

3 Open the same app on another Apple device, e.g. an iPad. The item created on your iPhone should be available to view and edit. Any changes will then show up on the file on your iPhone too

Continuing an email

1 Create an email on your iPhone and tap on **Cancel**

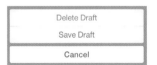

2 Tap on **Save Draft**

3 Open the Mail app on another Apple device. The email will be available in the **Drafts** folder and can be continued here

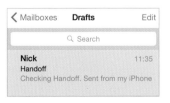

About Family Sharing

As everyone gets more and more digital devices, it is becoming increasingly important to be able to share content with other people, particularly family members. In iOS 9, the Family Sharing function enables you to share items that you have downloaded from the App Store, such as music and movies, with up to six other family members, as long as they have an Apple ID. Once this has been set up it is also possible to share items such as family calendars, photos and even see where family members are using Maps. To set up and start using Family Sharing:

1 Access the iCloud section within the Settings app, as shown on page 52

2 Tap on the **Set Up Family Sharing** button

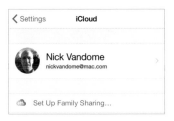

3 Tap on the **Get Started** button

4 One person will be the organizer of Family Sharing, i.e. in charge of it, and if you set it up then it will be you. Tap on the **Continue** button (the Family Sharing account will then be linked to your Apple ID)

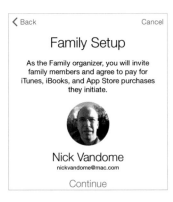

5   Tap on the **Continue** button again

6   If you are the organizer of Family Sharing, payments for items will be taken from the credit/debit card that you registered when you set up your Apple ID. Tap on the **Continue** button to confirm this

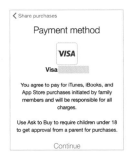

7   Once Family Sharing has been created, return to the iCloud section in the Settings app and tap on the **Add Family Member...** button

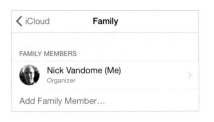

8   Enter the name or email address of a family member and tap on the **Next** button

9   An invitation is sent to the selected person. They have to accept this before they can participate in Family Sharing

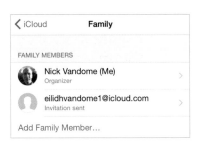

When you invite a family member you have an option for requiring them to ask for permission whenever they want to download anything from the App Store or the iTunes Store. This is usually done for children that are part of Family Sharing.

Using Family Sharing

Once you have set up Family Sharing and added family members, you can start sharing a variety of items.

Sharing Photos

Photos can be shared with Family Sharing thanks to the Family album that is created automatically within the Photos app. To use this and share photos:

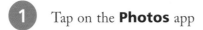

1 Tap on the **Photos** app

2 Tap the **Shared** button

3 The **Family** album is already available in the **Shared** section. Tap on the cloud button to access the album and start adding photos to it

Family
Shared by You

4 Tap on this button to add photos to the album

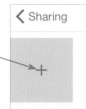

5 Tap on the photos you want to add and then tap on the **Done** button

6 Make sure the **Family** album is selected as the Shared Album and then tap on the **Post** button

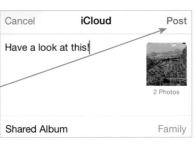

Beware

iCloud Photo Sharing has to be turned **On** to enable Family Sharing (**Settings > Photos & Camera > iCloud Photo Sharing**).

Hot tip

When someone else in your Family Sharing circle adds a photo to the Family album, you are notified in the Notification Center and also by a red notification on the Photos app.

...cont'd

Finding family members

Family Sharing makes it easy to keep in touch with the rest of the family and see exactly where they are. This can be done with the Find Friends app. The other person must have their iPhone or iPad (or other Apple device) turned on and online. To find family members:

1 Locate and download the **Find Friends** app in the App Store

2 Open the Find Friends app to display all of the active Family Sharing devices. Tap once on a person's name to view their details and location. Tap on your own name and check that the **Share My Location** button is **On**

To use Find Friends, all family members, or friends, must have iOS 8 (or later) or OS X Yosemite (or later) installed as the operating system on their device. They also need to have shared their location, as in Step 2 here.

Sharing music, videos, apps and books

Family Sharing means that all members of the group can share purchases from the iTunes Store, the App Store or the iBooks store. To do this:

1 Open either **iTunes Store**, **App Store** or **iBooks**

2 Tap on the **Purchased** button (can be accessed from the **More** button)

3 Tap on a member of the Family Sharing group

4 The person's purchases are listed. Tap on a category to view those purchases and download them to your iPhone, if required

When Family Sharing is set up, a Family calendar is created in the Calendar app. This can be used to add events that can be seen by everyone in the Family Sharing group.

Backing Up with iTunes

The iPhone and iOS 9 are both very much linked to the online world, and the iCloud service can be used to store and synchronize several types of content. However, it is still possible to use iTunes on a Mac or PC to sync content, including:

- Music

- Videos

- Apps

- TV shows

- Podcasts

- Books

iTunes can be used to sync these items (or some of them) onto your iPhone. To do this:

1 Connect your iPhone to your computer. iTunes should open automatically but if it does not, launch it in the usual way. Click on your iPhone at the top left-hand corner of the iTunes window. Click on the **Summary** tab to view general details about your iPhone

2 iTunes can also be used to back up your iPhone (in addition to iCloud). To do this, click on the **This computer** button under the **Automatically Back Up** section or click on the **Back Up Now** button

3 Click on the tabs in the left-hand panel to select the items that you want to sync. These include Apps, Music, Movies, TV Shows, Podcasts, Books, Audiobooks and Photos

4 Select what you want to sync for each heading (this can be for items in a category or selected items)

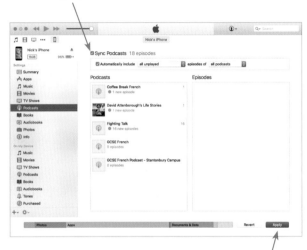

When you are syncing items to your iPad it is best to select specific folders or files, rather than including everything. This is because items such as music, videos and photos can take up a lot of storage space on your iPad if you sync a large library from your computer.

63

5 Click on the **Apply** button to start the sync process and copy the selected items to your iPhone

6 On the **Summary** page, scroll down to view the **Options** for syncing, such as specifying only checked songs and videos to be synced, or

Options

☑ Automatically sync when this iPhone is connected
☐ Sync with this iPhone over Wi-Fi
☑ Sync only checked songs and videos
☐ Prefer standard definition videos
☐ Convert higher bit rate songs to [128 kbps ⌄] AAC
☐ Manually manage videos
[Reset Warnings]
[Configure Accessibility...]

manually manage your videos for syncing

Backing Up with iCloud

Another backing up option is one that only needs to be set up once and then you do not have to worry about it again, because the backup happens automatically. This is done through iCloud and it can be set up in the iCloud settings. To do this:

1 Tap on the **Settings** app

2 Tap on the **iCloud** button

3 Tap on the **Backup** button

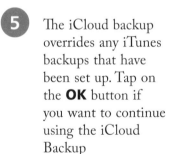

Hot tip

iCloud backups can be used to restore your data when you buy a new iPhone or if you need to reset it for any reason and erase all of its data: **Settings > General > Reset > Erase All Content and Settings**.

64

4 Drag the **iCloud Backup** button to **On**

5 The iCloud backup overrides any iTunes backups that have been set up. Tap on the **OK** button if you want to continue using the iCloud Backup

6 iCloud will perform automatic backups periodically when the iPhone is locked, connected to Wi-Fi and plugged in, e.g. for charging. Tap on the **Back Up Now** button to perform a manual backup

3 The Phone Functions

In this chapter we will look at how to use the phone functions to make and receive calls, maintain contact lists and make video calls using FaceTime.

Answering Calls

When you receive a call the iPhone will either ring or vibrate, depending on your iPhone settings. If the iPhone is locked, you will see the name of the caller on the screen and you will need to slide to unlock the phone and answer the call. If the iPhone is unlocked when the call comes in, you will be given the option to **Accept** or **Decline** (and send to voicemail).

When you receive an incoming call, you can answer by tapping on the green **Accept** button.

If you do not want to take the call and let it go to voicemail, tap on **Decline** or tap on the **Remind Me** button to be sent a reminder about the missed call at a certain time.

Tap on the **Message** button to send a text message to the person phoning.

Don't forget

After answering a call, the options on the Home screen include: muting the call; accessing the phone's keypad; putting the call on speaker; adding another call; making a FaceTime video call to the person (if they have a compatible device, otherwise it will not be available); and adding the caller to your contacts.

After answering a call you will see the various options available.

Tap on the red button to end a call.

Decline

Making Calls Using the Keypad

Although you can do a multitude of things with the iPhone, one of its basic functions is making phone calls. To do this:

1 Tap on the **Phone** app

2 Select the keypad icon. This brings up a standard keypad on the touchscreen

Keypad

Don't forget

If you enter a number that belongs to an existing contact, the contact's name will appear beneath the number once it has been entered.

3 Dial the number. This appears at the top of the screen as you add it

Make FaceTime Video Calls

To use FaceTime

- The caller and recipient must both use an iPhone 4 or later

- Alternatively, you can use a FaceTime-enabled Mac or iPad

- FaceTime calls can only be made using Wi-Fi or Cellular

The FaceTime settings

Don't forget

FaceTime also has to be turned **On** in the **FaceTime** section of the **Settings** app.

Don't forget

You can also make a FaceTime call to someone by selecting them in the **Contacts** app and tapping the FaceTime icon.

1 Tap on the FaceTime app

2 Tap on this button to select a contact

3 Select a contact to call. This will be from the Contacts app

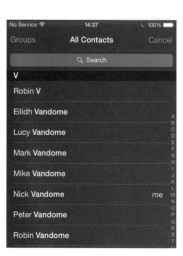

4 For the selected contact, tap on this button to make the FaceTime call

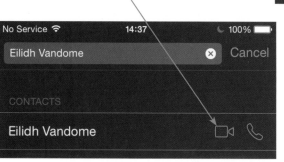

5 While the call is being accepted your own image appears in the main window

6 The recipient must tap **Accept**

7 Once the call has been connected, the recipient's image appears in the main window

If you have already had a FaceTime video call with someone, you can go to **Recents** and make another FaceTime call.

Actions during a FaceTime call

1 Tap on this button to mute the call. You will still be able to see the caller

2 Tap on this button to toggle between the front and back cameras

3 Tap on this button to end a FaceTime call

Using the Contacts List

The Contacts app acts like your own address book on the iPhone:

1 Tap the **Contacts** app on the Home screen

2 Flick up or down until you find the contact you wish to call. Tap on a contact's name

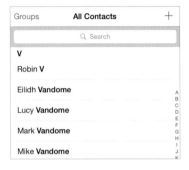

3 Select the action you wish to take, e.g. send a text message, make a FaceTime call, or phone the contact. Tap on the relevant icon to perform that task

The add photo function can also be used to edit an existing photo, or delete it.

Add photo to contact

If you want to assign a photo to a contact, access the contact, tap **Edit** and tap **add photo** (or **edit**) next to their name. Select a photo or take a new one. This gives a more personalized phone call, instead of just seeing a name or a number on the screen.

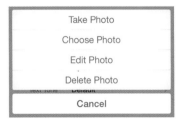

70

Using the Favorites List

People you call regularly can be added to your Favorites list. This is the first icon (from the left) when you open the phone application.

To add someone to your Favorites list

1 Open **Contacts**

2 Select the contact you wish to add

3 Tap **Add to Favorites** at the bottom of the window

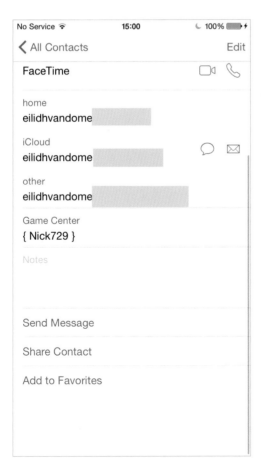

Add the contacts you call most to your Favorites list.

Recents List

Recent calls you have made or missed are listed under Recents.

Missed calls

● These are in the **Missed** tab and are listed in red

● **All** shows the calls made, received and missed

● Calls made are shown by this icon

● Calls received are shown without an icon

Hot tip

If someone has left you a voicemail message this is indicated by a solid red dot on the **Phone** app and also on the **Voicemail** button on the bottom toolbar of the Phone app. Tap on the **Voicemail** button to listen to your messages.

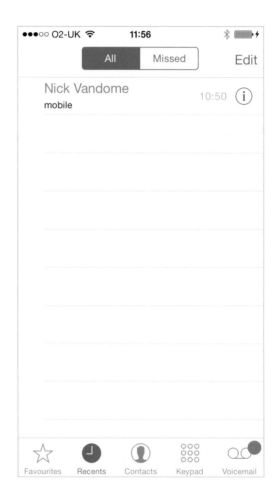

To return a call using Recents list

From the names shown in the Recents list, simply tap the name of the person you wish to call.

Assigning Ringtones

The iPhone has a number of polyphonic ringtones built in, or you can buy more from iTunes or even make your own. You can have the default tone for every caller or you can assign a specific tone for a contact.

To assign a ringtone

1 Tap on the **Phone** app

2 Tap on Contacts and select a contact, then click **Edit**

3 Click on the **Ringtone** link

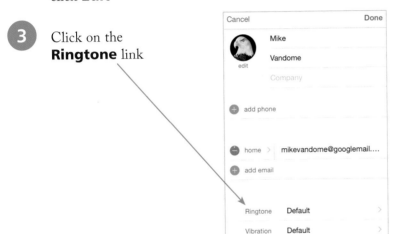

4 Choose the ringtone you wish to assign and tap on the **Done** button

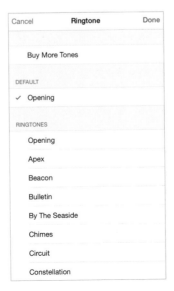

Do Not Disturb

There are times when you do not want to see or hear notifications from apps, or receive phone calls. For example, during the night you may want to divert all calls to voicemail rather than be woken up by phone calls.

1 Open **Settings > Do Not Disturb**

2 Slide the slider to **On** if you want to switch on Do Not Disturb

Allow some callers to get through

You may want to allow friends and family, or those in your Favorites list to get through and not be diverted to voicemail.

1 Open **Settings > Do Not Disturb**

2 Choose the scheduled time (if you wish to schedule)

3 **Allow Calls From >** choose **Everyone, No One, Favorites**, or specific groups

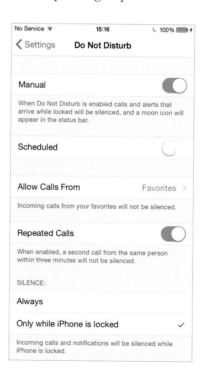

Missed Calls

It happens to all of us from time to time: someone calls and somehow you manage to miss it. If your iPhone was locked when the call was made you can see at a glance that a call was missed, denoted by the red icon on the Phone app.

You can find out exactly when the call was made by looking at the missed calls list:

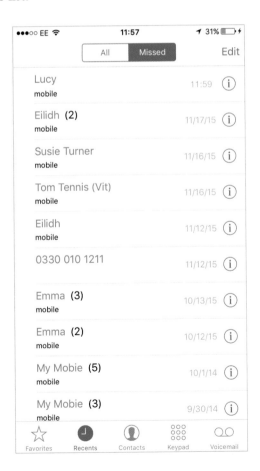

Make the Most of Contacts

The Contacts application on the iPhone lets you call someone, send them an SMS or MMS, email them, and assign them specific ringtones.

Add someone to Contacts
If you get a call from someone who is not in your contacts list, you can add them from the Phone app.

Try to enter as much contact information as possible, since this gives you more options for contacting them.

1 Open the Phone app and tap on the **Recents** button on the bottom toolbar

2 Recent calls and their numbers will be displayed

3 Select a number and tap on the **Create New Contact** button

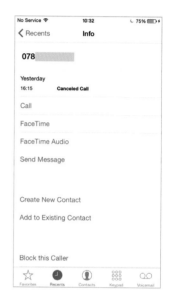

4 Enter the details for the contact and tap on the **Done** button. The contact's details will be added to the Contacts app

76

Adding Contacts

You can also add contacts directly into the Contacts app, so you can then access their details. To do this:

1 Tap on the **Contacts** app

2 Tap on the **+** button to add details for a new contact

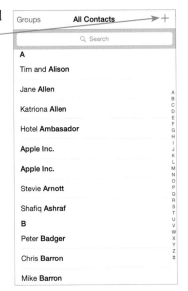

3 Enter the details for the contact, including First and Last Name, Phone, Email and Address. Tap on the **add photo** button to browse to a photo, or take one with the camera. Tap on the green **+** buttons to include extra items for each field

4 Tap on the **Done** button. The contact's details will be added to the Contacts app

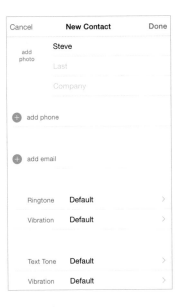

Deleting Contacts

It is relatively easy to delete contacts:

1 Tap the contact you wish to remove

2 Once their details are loaded, tap **Edit** at the top right

Your contacts can also be accessed and managed through your iCloud online account (**www.icloud.com**), if you have set one up, using an Apple ID.

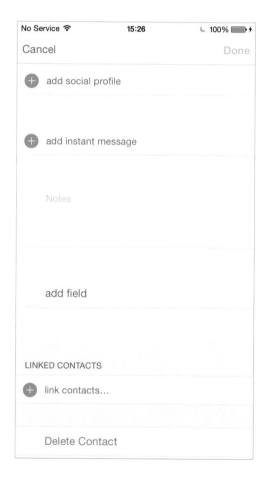

3 Scroll down to the bottom of the screen and tap **Delete Contact**

4 That's it!

Making Calls Using Headphones

You don't have to hold the iPhone to your ear each time you want to make a call. It is often more convenient to use the headphones. This means you can keep the phone on the desk and make notes during the call.

The headphones are very sophisticated – the right cord contains a white rectangular button which is useful when listening to music – but they are also great for making calls.

How to use the headphones

Make a phone call	Dial as normal and speak normally. You will hear the caller via the headphones and they will hear your voice, which is picked up by the inbuilt microphone
Answer a call	Click the middle of the control button once
Decline a call	Press the middle of the controller and hold for ~two seconds (you will hear two low beeps to confirm)
End call	Press the middle of the controller once
If already on a call and you wish to switch to an incoming call and put current call on hold	Press the middle button once to talk to Caller 2 (and press again to bring Caller 1 back)
Switch to incoming call and end the current call	Press and hold the middle of the controller for ~two seconds (you will hear two low beeps to confirm)
Use Voice Control to dial the number	Press and hold the middle button and say the number or the contact's name

Beware

You can use third party headphones with the iPhone but it is likely you may lose some functionality.

Hide or Show Your Caller ID

Sometimes you do not want the person you are calling to know your iPhone phone number. You can easily hide your number so it does not display on their screen.

1 Go to **Settings > Phone > Show My Caller ID**

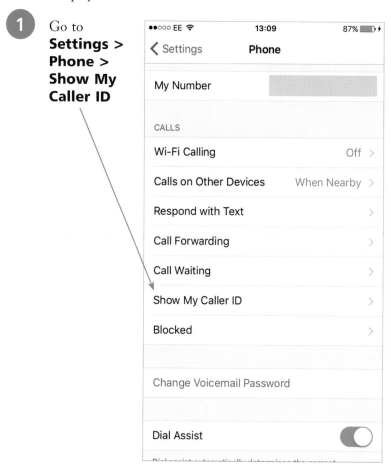

2 Tap Show My Caller ID **On** or **Off** depending on whether or not you want it to show

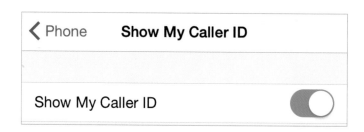

Call Forwarding

Sometimes you need to forward calls from your iPhone to another phone. For example, if you are somewhere with no cell phone coverage. This is pretty straightforward.

Setting up call forwarding

1 Go to **Settings > Phone > Call Forwarding**

2 Slide the **Call Forwarding** button to the right (**On**)

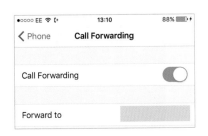

3 You will be asked for the number you wish to forward calls to

4 When you no longer need to have your calls forwarded, go back and switch it off

Activate call forwarding if you cannot access the iPhone. You could forward to a landline or a work colleague.

Conference Calls

This allows you to talk to more than one person at a time and is much like making conference calls using a landline.

Make a conference call

1 Make a call

2 Tap the **add call** icon on the screen

3 The first call is put on hold

4 Select another contact and make a call to them

5 Tap **Merge Calls**

6 Now, everyone can hear each other

7 Repeat until up to five people are on the same call

Call Waiting

What is the value of Call Waiting? If Call Waiting is switched off, and someone phones you while you are on a call, they will be put straight through to voicemail. However, if Call Waiting is activated, they will know your line is busy and can wait until you are off the call. Or you can answer their call and put the first caller on hold.

1 Go to **Settings > Phone**

2 Tap **Call Waiting**

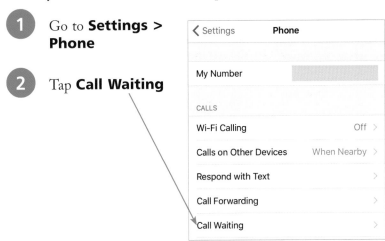

3 Slide the **Off** button to the **On** position

iPhone Usage Data

How many SMS messages do you have left this month? Or talk minutes? There are times when you need to monitor your usage, since exceeding your limits on your contracted allowance will cost you extra.

How can you check how much you have used?
The iPhone has Usage data under **Settings > Cellular (Mobile Data)**. The information here is fairly limited in terms of what you have used, or have left, in this month's cycle.

If you exceed your monthly allowance on the iPhone you will be charged extra.

There are some great third party apps that help you monitor your monthly cellular, Wi-Fi and data usage. Look for these in the App Store.

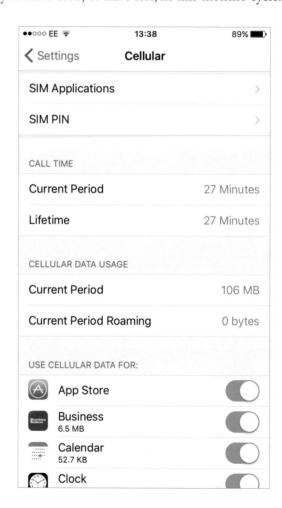

Third party applications
There are a number of apps that can track your monthly usage. These include *Optus Mobile Usage* for the US and *Allowance* for the UK. Other countries will have their own specific apps.

4 Messaging

Sending text and multimedia messages is no longer a chore. The iPhone *carries out these functions effortlessly, and this chapter shows how to use the Messages app for all of your messaging needs.*

Text Messaging

Sending text messages on the iPhone 6s is a fast and efficient way to communicate using your iPhone. You can send messages as SMS (simple message system), MMS (multimedia message system – basically text with pictures, see page 90), and iMessage.

SMS

Hot tip

You can send SMS, MMS and iMessages to multiple recipients. Simply add additional names in the **To:** box when you create the message, as in Step 3.

Don't forget

SMS and MMS messages are sent over your mobile carrier's network. iMessages are sent to other Apple users with an Apple ID, using Wi-Fi.

Don't forget

Message settings can be specified in **Settings > Messages**. These include options for sending Read Receipts so that you are notified when someone reads your message.

1 Tap the **Messages** app on the Home screen

2 Tap the **New message** icon at the top right of the screen

3 Enter a recipient name or a phone number in the **To:** box

4 Add any other names if you wish to send to more than one person

5 Go to the **text box** at the bottom and enter your message

6 Hit **Send**

7 The progress bar will show you the status of the message

8 Once sent, your message will appear in a green speech bubble (blue if iMessage)

9 Once the recipient replies, you will see their message below yours in a white speech bubble

iMessage

You can send iMessages using cellular or Wi-Fi to other people with iOS devices (or Macs). Simply send your text in the usual way. You will know it's an iMessage rather than SMS because your message will be in a blue speech bubble. You can also check the status of your text message (Delivered or Read) by checking below your message.

You can tell this message is an iMessage – you see iMessage at the top, plus my text is in a blue speech bubble. You can also see that my message was successfully delivered. If you see the **...** ellipsis in a speech bubble on the left, the person you texted is writing a reply.

Assign SMS messages a specific notification sound so you know you have received an SMS. This can be done in **Settings > Sounds > Text Tone** and select the sound you want to use.

To see how many characters you have used go to **Settings > Messages > Character Count > On**. 160 characters is the limit for one SMS.

Sometimes things go wrong; maybe you entered a wrong digit, and the message does not get sent, indicated by a red exclamation mark next to it. You can amend the number or tap on the red exclamation mark and tap on **Try Again**.

Using Predictive Text

Predictive text tries to guess what you are typing and also predict the next word following the one you have just typed. It is excellent for text messaging and it is available with the iPhone 6s with iOS 9. To use it:

1 Tap on the **General** tab in the Settings app

 General

2 Tap on the **Keyboard** link

 Keyboard >

3 Drag the **Predictive** button **On**

 Predictive

4 When predictive text is activated, the QuickType bar is displayed above the keyboard. Initially, this has a suggestion for the first word to include. Tap on a word or start typing

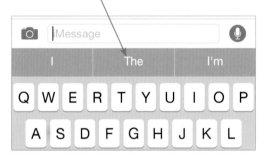

Predictive text learns from your writing style as you write and so gets more accurate at predicting words. It can also recognize a change in style for different apps, such as Mail and Messages.

5 As you type, suggestions appear. Tap on one to accept it. Tap on the word within the quotation marks to accept exactly what you have typed

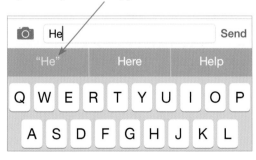

6 If you continue typing, the predictive suggestions will change as you add more letters

7 After you have typed a word, a suggestion for the next word appears. Tap on one of the suggestions, or start typing a new word, which will then also have predictive suggestions as you type

Toggling predictive text from the keyboard

You can also toggle predictive text On or Off from the keyboard. To do this:

1 Press on this button on the keyboard

2 Tap on the **Predictive** button to turn it **On** or **Off**

Hot tip

The button in Step 1 can also be used to add Emojis (or smileys) which are symbols used in text messages to signify happiness, surprise, sadness, etc.

Sending MMS Messages

The iPhone can send more than just plain, boring text messages. MMS means Multimedia Message Service, which is basically a means of sending images, including video, to a recipient, rather than a simple SMS message. Each MMS counts as two SMS messages, so be careful how many you send.

To send an MMS

MMS messages sometimes incur charges with cellular/mobile phone carriers. Check with your provider if you are in doubt.

1 Tap **Messages** and tap the **New message** icon

2 Enter the **name** of the recipient

3 Tap the **camera** icon (to the left of the text box)

4 Tap on the **Take Photo or Video** button to capture a new image, or tap on the **Photo Library** button to select an item from your photos or videos

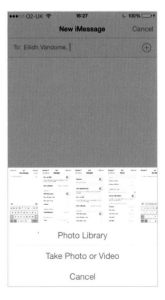

5 Browse to the picture or video you want to send, from within the **Photos** app, and tap on the **Choose** button to select it

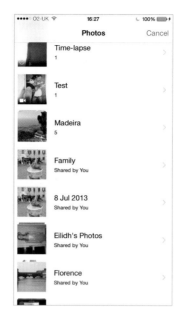

6 The picture will appear in the message box

7 Type your text message to accompany the picture or video

8 Hit **Send**

Sending Audio Clips

You can also send audio messages in an iMessage so that people can actually hear from you too. To do this:

Recipients will need to have a compatible phone or computer in order to play an audio message.

1 Open a new iMessage

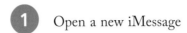
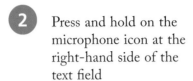

2 Press and hold on the microphone icon at the right-hand side of the text field

3 Create your audio clip and release the microphone button

4 Tap on this button to add the clip to the message

5 Tap on this button to delete the current clip and start recording again

6 If the audio clip is added it shows up in the iMessages area. The recipient can use the **Play** button to hear it

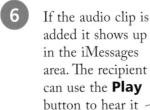
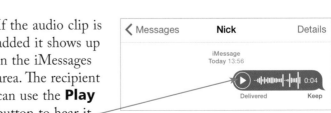

Sharing Your Location

With Messages you can now also show people your location (by sending a map) rather than just telling them. To do this:

1 Open a conversation where someone has asked where you are, tap once on the **Details** button

2 Tap once on the **Details** button

3 Tap once on the **Send My Current Location**, or **Share My Location** buttons

4 For Share My Location, tap once on one of the options for how long you want your location to be shared for. These include sharing for an hour, a day or indefinitely

5 Your location is shown on a map and sent to the other person in the conversation

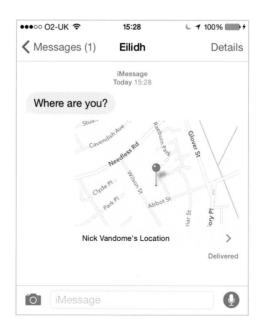

If you select **Share My Location**, this will be updated if your location changes (as long as Location Services is turned **On** in **Settings > Privacy > Location Services**.

Managing Text Messages

Forwarding a text message

You can easily forward a text message to another person.

1 Open the message and press and hold on the message

2 Tap on the **More** button

3 Tap on the **Forward** button and enter a recipient name

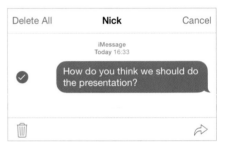

Deleting a text message

1 Open Messages to show your list of text messages

2 Swipe the text message left to right then tap **Delete**

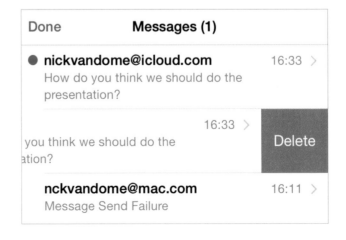

In the App Store there are several apps that let you message friends and colleagues. Examples include Skype, WhatsApp, Viber, and others.

Skype

Viber

Editing text messages

You can selectively delete parts of a text message thread:

1 Open the message and press and hold on the message

2 Tap on the **More** button

3 Tap next to a message to select it

4 To delete the selected messages tap on the **Trash** icon

Tap on the **Delete All** button to delete all of the messages in a conversation.

Live Links

When you send a text message, an email, or use a social networking app where text is inserted, you can add phone numbers, web URLs and email addresses. The recipient can then click on these to return the call, visit a website, or send an email.

SMS with telephone number
Tap on a phone number in a message to call it.

Phone numbers, email addresses and URLs in messages are live and can be tapped to call the number, view other web pages or send emails.

SMS with email address
Tap on an email address in a message to create an email to that person.

Hot tip

Live links to phone numbers and email addresses don't end with Mail. You can also use phone numbers in Safari. If you see a number you want to dial on a web page, put your finger on the number and hold until a box pops up showing you the various options. These include calling the number, sending a text message, creating a new contact or adding to an existing contact.

Live links in emails
If you send an email to someone and include a website, email address or URL these are also clickable.

Click on the link to go to that site in a web browser.

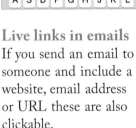

5 Music and Movies

The iPhone *is a workhorse, but is also a fun device, able to play music and movies with excellent sound quality and superb visual quality on the Retina HD screen. This chapter shows how to obtain, play and manage music on your* iPhone *and also view movies and other similar content from the* iTunes Store.

The Music App

The music app can be used to turn your iPhone into your own personal jukebox. To use it:

 Tap on the **Music** app on the Dock

 Tap on the **My Music** button on the bottom toolbar. This displays any music items that you have bought from the iTunes Store (see page 104) or downloaded from the Apple Music service (see pages 102-103)

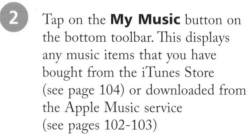

Tap on the **Artists** button to view more options for how you view your music, such as by Albums, Songs, Genres and Composers

Artists ⌄

Play Audio on the Music App

The Music app is very versatile for playing your favorite albums and tracks. To use it:

1   Tap on the **Music** app on the Dock

2   Tap on the **Library** button at the top of the window and tap **Artists**, or one of the categories as shown in Step 3 on the previous page

Tap on this bar to search for items in alphabetical order. Tap on the Search icon at the top of the window to search for specific artists or songs.

3   Tap the name of the artist and choose the album you want to hear (tap on the **My Music** button to move back to the previous screen)

4   Tap on the track that you want to play. If you select the first track of an album then the other tracks will play in sequence after it

You can play a song from your music library by using Siri. Hold down the Home button until Siri appears and then say, 'Play, (name of song)' and it should start playing automatically.

Music App Controls

Once a track is playing in the Music app there are a number of controls that can be used.

1 Tap here to view the selected track playing in the Music app interface

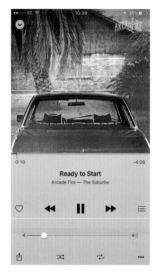

The volume can also be changed using the controls on the iPhone headphones (see page 36), or with the volume button on the side of the iPhone.

Music controls, including Play, Fast Forward, Rewind and Volume can also be applied in the **Control Center**, which can be accessed by swiping up from the bottom of the screen.

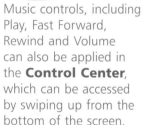

2 Tap once on the middle button to pause/play the currently-playing track. Use the buttons on either side to move to the beginning or end of a track

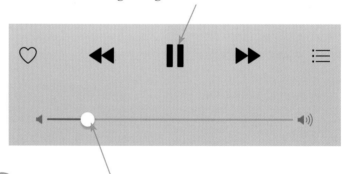

3 Drag this button to increase or decrease the volume

4 Tap once on this button to repeat a song or album after it has played

5 Tap once on this button to shuffle the order of songs on your iPhone

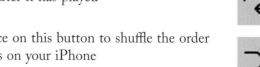

View the Music Tracks

Sometimes you want to see what tracks are available while you are listening to audio, or download tracks.

While viewing the album artwork screen
To view the Up Next tracks:

1 Tap on this button at the right of the music controls screen

2 The **Up Next** tracks are displayed, e.g. the rest of the current album. To get back to the main screen again, tap on the **Done** button at the top right

Downloading tracks
To download tracks that have been bought through iTunes on another device (or Apple Music):

1 Tap on this button

2 Tap on **Make Available Offline** to download an album or an individual track

Items that are in your iTunes Library but have not been bought on your iPhone, e.g. bought on an iPad, are played on your iPhone by streaming over Wi-Fi. This means that the actual item is not downloaded to your iPhone, unless you use the **Make Available Offline** option.

101

Starting with Apple Music

Apple Music is a new service that makes the entire Apple iTunes Library of music available to users. It is a subscription service, but there is a three-month free trial. Music can be streamed over the internet or downloaded so you can listen to it when you are offline. To start with Apple Music:

1 Tap once on the **Music** app

2 Tap once on the **For You** button

3 Tap once on the **Start 3 Month Free Trial** button. (Either an **Individual** or a **Family** membership plan can be selected, and your Apple ID Password is required to sign-in)

4 Select the types of music in which you are interested and tap once on the **Next** button to move through the process. This will help to populate the **For You** page, which is a selection of suggestions which you may like. You can also search for items using the Search icon at the top of the Apple Music window

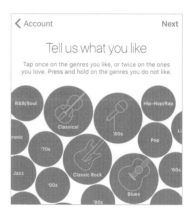

Using Apple Music

Once you have registered for Apple Music you can begin accessing and playing the huge music resource that is available. To do this:

1 Tap once on an item to display it. Tap once on individual tracks to play them (by streaming)

By default, music from Apple Music is stored within iCloud and this is where it is streamed from. This means that it is played over an online Wi-Fi connection. If it is downloaded, as in Step 2, then it can be played even if you are not online.

2 Tap once here to access the menu for a track or album. Tap once on the **Make Available Offline** button to download the item to your **My Music** library

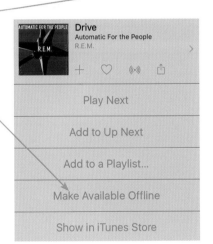

103

For Apple Music to work properly, both **Show Apple Music** and **iCloud Music Library** should be turned **On** within the **Music** section of the **Settings** app.

3 Tap once on the **My Music** button on the bottom toolbar

4 The item is added to your **My Music** page and can be accessed here, even if you are not online and connected directly to the Apple Music service

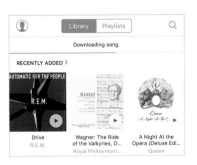

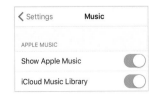

Buying Music

Music on the iPhone can be downloaded and played using the iTunes and Music apps respectively. iTunes links to the iTunes Store, from where music and other content can be bought and downloaded to your iPhone. To do this:

1 Tap once on the **iTunes Store** app

2 Tap once on the **Music** button on the iTunes toolbar at the bottom of the window

3 Use the buttons at the bottom of the window to view the music content, or swipe up and down, and left and right in the main window

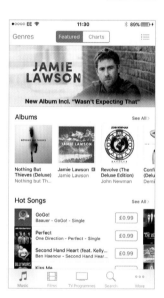

Beware

You need to have an Apple ID with credit or debit card details added to be able to buy music from the iTunes Store.

104

4 Tap once on an item to view it. Tap once here to buy an album or tap on the button next to a song to buy that individual item

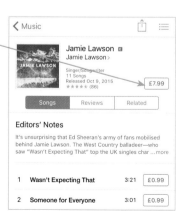

5 Purchased items are included in the Music app's Library

Watching Movies

The iPhone is a great video player.

1. Tap on the **Videos** app

2. To find content, tap on the **Store** button

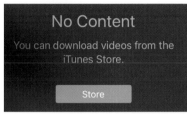

3. Browse the video store to select a title and download it

4. Select the video in the **Videos** app and tap the **Play** button. The playback screen will automatically rotate to landscape

5. Adjust volume, rewind and access other features using the controls which are shown below

6. If you want to stop, simply press the **Play/Pause** button and it will save your place

You can also watch YouTube videos on your iPhone, by either going to the YouTube website in Safari, or by downloading the YouTube app from the App Store.

You have a few ways of getting videos on your iPhone: home movies, either using a camcorder or the iPhone camera; convert your purchased DVDs to iPhone format; and buying or renting movies from the iTunes Store. DVDs can be converted with an app such as Handbrake, but make sure it is legal to do so first.

Podcasts

The iPhone is also great for listening to audiobooks and podcasts. This can be done with the Podcasts app that can be downloaded from the App Store.

1 Open the **Podcasts** app

2 Tap on the Podcasts app to open it and view the available podcasts (which can be audio and video)

3 Tap on a podcast to download it to your iPhone

4 Tap on a podcast in the **My Podcasts** section to listen to it. If a podcast has a red circle on it with a number, this means that there are updates or new versions/episodes available for it

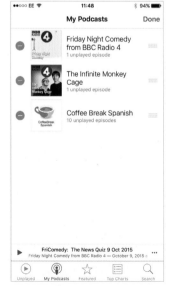

6 Photos and Videos

The iPhone *has two built-in cameras, and is able to shoot video as well as still images. In addition, you can manage and edit your photos and videos directly on the* iPhone *itself, with the Photos app.*

Sharing Content

Since the iPhone can store and create such a great range of content, it seems a shame to keep it all to yourself as there are options for sharing all kinds of content. The example here is for one of the most popular, sharing photos, but the process also applies to other content such as web pages, notes and contacts.

1 Open a photo at full size and tap on the **Share** button

2 Tap on one of the options for sharing the photo. These include messaging, emailing, sending to iCloud, sending to a note, adding to a contact in your Contacts app, using as your iPhone wallpaper, tweeting, sending to Facebook or Flickr, printing and copying

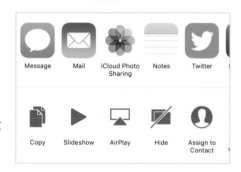

3 The photo is added to the item selected in Step 2, in this case an iMessage in the Messages app

Sharing with AirDrop

AirDrop is a feature for sharing files wirelessly with other Apple users over short distances. It has been available on Mac computers for a number of years and is available on the iPhone 6s. To use it:

1 Swipe up from the bottom of the screen to open the Control Center, to activate AirDrop

2 Tap on the **AirDrop** link

3 Select how you want to share your files with other AirDrop users. This can be with your contacts in the Contacts app, or Everyone

4 Select an item you want to share, such as a photo in the Photos app, and tap on the **Share** button

5 If there are people nearby with AirDrop activated, the AirDrop button will be blue on your iPhone

6 Tap on an available icon to share your content with this person (they will have to accept it via AirDrop once it has been sent)

Other types of content can be shared with AirDrop, but photos are one of the most common.

When using AirDrop, make sure you are as close as possible to the other user and that they have AirDrop turned on in the Control Center.

Where Are My Pictures?

As shown in Chapter One, the iSight camera can be used to capture photos and video. Once these have been captured they can be viewed and organized in the Photos app. To do this:

1 Tap on the **Photos** app

If you have iCloud set up for photos, select **Settings > Photos & Camera** and turn On **Upload to My Photo Stream** to enable all of your new photos taken on your iPhone to be made available on any other iCloud-enabled devices. Turn On **iCloud Photo Library** to make your photos on other devices available on your iPhone too.

2 At the top level, all photos are displayed according to the years in which they were taken

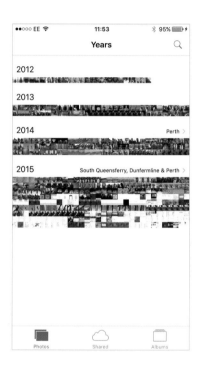

Tap once on the **Photos**, **Shared** and **Albums** buttons at the bottom of the **Years**, **Collections** or **Moments** windows, to view the photos in each of these sections.

3 Tap within the **Years** window to view photos according to specific, more defined, timescales. This is the **Collections** level. Tap on the **Years** button to move back up one level

4 Tap within the **Collections** window to drill down further into the photos, within the **Moments** window. Tap on the **Collections** button to go back up one level

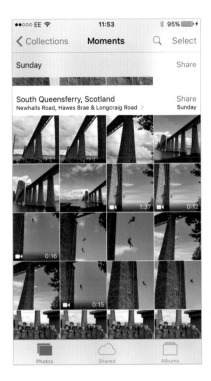

Moments are created according to the time at which the photos were added or taken: photos added at the same time will be displayed within the same Moment.

5 Tap on a photo within the **Moments** window to view it at full size. Tap on the **Moments** button to go back up one level

Double-tap with one finger on an individual photo to zoom in on it. Double-tap with one finger again to zoom back out. To zoom in to a greater degree, spread outwards with thumb and forefinger.

Creating Albums

Within the Photos app it is possible to create different albums in which you can store photos. This can be a good way to organize them according to different categories and headings. To do this:

1 Tap on the **Albums** button

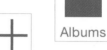

2 Tap on this button

3 Enter a name for the new album

4 Tap on the **Save** button

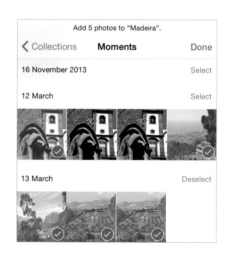

New Album
Enter a name for this album.

Madeira

Cancel   Save

Don't forget

When photos are placed into albums, the originals remain in the main **Photos** section.

5 Tap on the photos you want to include in the album

6 Tap on the **Done** button

Done

Add 5 photos to "Madeira".

‹ Collections   **Moments**   Done

16 November 2013   Select

12 March   Select

13 March   Deselect

7 Tap on the **Albums** button to view the album

Madeira
5   ›

Photos   Shared   Albums

Selecting Photos

It is easy to take hundreds, or even thousands of digital photos, and most of the time you will only want to use a selection of them. Within the Photos app it is possible to select individual photos so that you can share them, delete them or add them to albums.

1 Access the Moments section and tap on the **Select** button

2 Tap on the photos you want to select, or tap on the **Select** button again to select all of the photos

Press and hold on a photo to access an option to copy it, rather than selecting it.

3 Tap on the **Deselect** button if you want to remove the selection

To add items to an album, tap on this button in the **Moments** section.

Tap on photos to select them, then tap on the **Add To** button and select either an existing album or tap on the **New Album** link to create a new album, with the selected photos added to it.

4 Use these buttons to, from left to right, share the selected photos, delete them or add them to an album

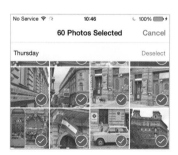

Editing Photos

The Photos app has options to perform some basic photo-editing operations. To use these:

1 Open a photo at full-screen size and tap once on the **Edit** button to access the editing tools

Edit

2 Tap on the **Auto Enhance** button at the top right of the screen to have auto-coloring editing effects applied to the photo

3 Tap on the **Crop** button and drag the resizing handles to select an area of the photo that you want to keep and discard the rest

4 Tap on the **Rotate** button to rotate the photo 90 degrees at a time, anti-clockwise

5 Tap on the **Filters** button to select special effects to be applied to the photo

6 Tap on the **Enhance** button to have auto-coloring editing applied to the photo

7 For each function, tap on the **Done** button to save the photo with the selected changes

Hot tip

If you reopen a photo that has been edited and closed, you have an option to **Revert** to its original state, before it was edited.

8 Tap on the **Cancel** button to quit the editing process

Taking Videos

To capture your own video footage:

1 Tap the **Camera** icon to load the app. The shutter will open to show the image view

2 Drag just above the shutter button until **Video** is showing

3 Tap on the red **Record** button

4 The **Record** button turns into a red square during filming

5 When you have finished, tap the Record button again. Your video will be saved in the **Photos** app

Don't forget

The iPhone 6s and 6s Plus can capture video in 4k format, which is higher quality than High Definition (HD).

Hot tip

Hold the phone in landscape mode when shooting video.

Hot tip

Videos are located in the Photos section within the **Photos** app.

Editing the Video

You can edit the video you have taken on a Mac, PC or directly on the iPhone itself.

1 Tap the **Photos** app

2 Access the video in the same way as for accessing photos

3 **Tap the video** to open it – the image can be viewed in portrait or landscape, but landscape is easier for trimming

4 **Touch the screen** and tap on the **Edit** button. The trimming timeline will be shown at the bottom of the screen

5 Decide what (if anything) you want to trim and drag the yellow sliders on the left and right until you have marked the areas you wish to trim

Hot tip

Video editing is now non-destructive, which means you can trim your video, but the original video clip is left intact.

117

6 Tap the yellow **Done** button at the bottom right of the screen and the unwanted video will be removed

7 Tap on the **Save as New Clip** button to save the edited clip

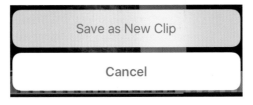

Hot tip

Tap on this button on the top toolbar so that it turns yellow, to activate Live Photos. This is a short animated clip that is captured in normal photo mode by tapping on the shutter button in Photo mode. It creates a short movie file that can be played in the Photos app by pressing and holding on it or send it to someone as a video. Tap on the button again to deactivate Live Photos.

Don't forget

Time-lapse shots are created like videos, with each frame that has been captured being played in sequence.

Creative Shots

The iPhone camera can also be used to create a range of video effects: you can create panorama, slow-motion shots or time-lapse effects. To do this:

Panoramas

1 For panoramas, open the **Camera** and select the **Pano** option by swiping along above the shutter button

2 Once you tap the shutter button (bottom of screen) you need to **pan from left to right keeping the arrow on the center line** for best results

Move iPhone continuously when taking a Panorama.

3 Once the arrow reaches the right side, the panoramic image will be created and saved in the Photos app (or tap this button to stop the panorama at that point)

Slow Motion

1 For slow-motion, select the **Slo-Mo** option and tap on the shutter button

2 The Slo-Mo option records video at 240 frames per second to create the slow motion effect

3 Tap the shutter button again to stop recording

Time-lapse

1 For time-lapse, select the **Time-lapse** option and tap on the shutter button

2 The camera keeps taking photos periodically until you press the shutter button again

7 The Standard Apps

Each iPhone *comes pre-installed with a*

core set of applications (apps), which make

it so versatile and useful. In this chapter

we explore some of the apps that haven't

been covered in other chapters and show

how to get the best use out of them.

Calendar

For those who want to get organized, people in business, education and many other sectors, the core Apple applications are: Calendar, Mail, Contacts, Phone and Notes.

These apps integrate well with each other on the iPhone and also on Mac computers with the same apps.

Setting up Calendar

Before you start entering data into Calendar, there are one or two settings you should check:

1 Go to **Settings > Mail, Contacts, Calendars**

2 Scroll down the page until you find **Calendars**

3 Tap **Time Zone Override** to override the automatic time zone

4 Choose what to **Sync** with iCloud. (Do you want all events or just those for the past two weeks, month, three months, or six months?)

5 Set your **Default Calendar** – when you make new appointments using Calendar this is where the appointments will be added. (You can add to another calendar quite easily, though.)

Beware

Make sure your Time Zone is set correctly or all of your appointments will be incorrect.

Hot tip

Turn Calendars **On** in iCloud (**Settings > iCloud**) to ensure your calendar events are saved to iCloud and so will be available on other iCloud-enabled devices.

120

●●○○○ EE 🗢   14:38   🖊 99% 🔋⚡

❮ Settings   **Mail, Contacts, Calendars**

Import SIM Contacts

CALENDARS

Time Zone Override   Off >

Alternate Calendars   Off >

Week Numbers ⚪

Show Invitee Declines 🔵

Sync   Events 1 Month Back >

Default Alert Times   >

Start Week On   >

Default Calendar   Birthdays >

Events Found in Mail 🔵

Turning this off will delete any unconfirmed event suggestions and prevent suggestions from appearing in the Calendar app.

Calendar Views

To start using Calendar:

1 Tap the **Calendar** icon to open the app

2 You will see the **Month View** – if it opens in **Day** or **List**, tap on the **Month** name at the top of the screen. This shows an overview of the month

3 A gray dot means you have an appointment on that day, but it does not tell you how long the appointment is or what it is. Tap on the dot and you will see what the day's appointments are

4 If you need a detailed view of your appointments, check out the **Day** view (see next page)

Back to year view

Today

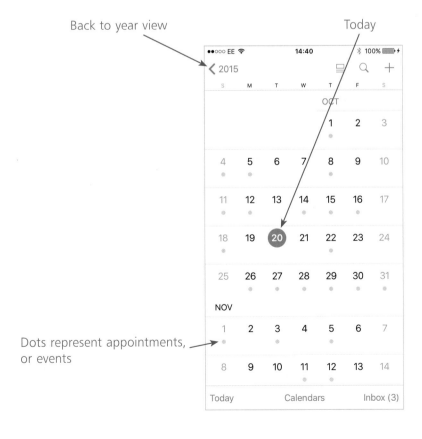

Dots represent appointments, or events

The Calendar uses continuous scrolling to move through Month view. This means you can view weeks across different months, rather than just viewing each month in its entirety, i.e. you can view the second half of one month and the first half of the next one in the same calendar window.

Tap on the **Today** button to view the calendar for the current day. From Day view, tap on the month button in the top left-hand corner to go to Month view. Tap on a date within the month to view it, with the days for the corresponding week at the top of the window. Swipe left and right on this to move between different weeks.

5 Tap on the **Today** button to view the calendar for the current day (tap on the red dot in Month view to go to that day). From Day view, tap on the month button in the top left-hand corner to go to Month view

Hot tip

To add more calendars, tap on the **Calendars** button and then the **Edit** button. Tap on the **Add Calendar** button at the bottom of the window and enter the required details.

6 Tap on a date within the month to view it, with the days for the corresponding week at the top of the window. Swipe left and right on this to move between different weeks

7 Tap on the **Calendars** button at the bottom of the window to view the available calendars

8 Tap on the **Inbox** button to view any invitations that you have been sent

9 Tap on the **List** button to view a scrollable list of all of your events

Searching Calendar

It's very easy to find appointments using the Search function within Calendar. You can also use the Spotlight search to find appointments.

1 Tap **Calendar** to open the app

2 Tap on the **List** button

3 Scroll through the appointments and then tap an appointment to see its details

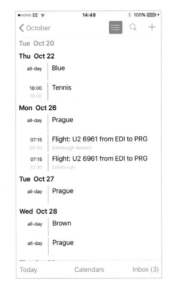

You can search your calendar using the inbuilt search tool or use Spotlight.

Spotlight Search

You can also search for appointments using the iPhone Spotlight search. To do this:

1 Swipe downwards anywhere on the Home screen to access the Spotlight search

2 Enter a search word or phrase. This will search over all of the content on your iPhone, including within Calendars

3 Tap on one of the entries under the **Events** heading in the search results

Adding Appointments

Set up new appointment

To create a new appointment, or event, in the Calendar app:

1 Tap on this button to create a new event or press and hold on a time slot

124

2 Enter a Title and a Location for the event

3 Drag the **All-day** button to Off to set a timescale for the event

4 Tap on the **Starts** button and drag on the barrels to set the time at which the appointment will start

5 Do the same for the **Ends** time of the appointment

6 Tap on the **Alert** button and select a time at which you want an alert about the appointment

You can also invite other people to an event using the Invitees button. People can also send you invites to events, in which case you will receive an invitation alert that will appear on the Home screen and also in the Notification Center. If you accept an invitation, it will be added to your calendar.

7 Tap on the **Calendar** button and select a calendar on which you would like the appointment to be included

8 Tap on the **Repeat** button and select a time for when you want the appointment or event to be repeated. This is a good option for items such as birthdays

Set up your repeat items, such as birthdays and anniversaries.

Keeping Notes

It is always useful to have a quick way of making notes of everyday things, such as shopping lists, recipes or packing lists for traveling. On your iPhone, the Notes app is perfect for this function. To use it:

1 Tap once on the **Notes** app

2 Tap once on this button to create a new note

3 Enter text for the note

4 Tap once on this button to share (via Message or Mail, or any social media apps on your iPhone), copy or print a note

●○○○○ EE 📶   14:41   100% 🔋⚡

❮ iCloud   ⬆️   Done

My latest note

5 Tap once on this button to access the formatting toolbar. Tap once on the cross to close the toolbar

6 Double-tap on text and tap once on this button to access text formatting options

7 Tap once on this button to create a bulleted checklist. Enter text for the list

8 Tap once on this button to add a handwritten, or stylus-drawn, item or drawing

9 Select a drawing object at the bottom of the screen and draw on the screen. Tap once on the **Done** button. The drawing is added to the current note

10 Tap once on this button to add a photo or video to a note. Select a photo or video from your library or take a new one

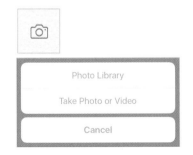

Press and hold firmly on the keyboard in Notes to activate it as a trackpad. You can then swipe over it to move the cursor around the screen. This can also be done in the Mail and Messages apps.

11 To save the note, tap **Done**, and then the latest note appears at the top of the iCloud list. Each time a note is edited it moves to the top

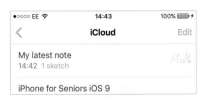

127

Maps App

Maps is a great application – it can help you find where you currently are, where you want to go, help you plan the route, tell you which direction you are facing and where all the traffic is. To use maps:

Maps will only work with its full functionality if **Location Services** is switched **On**.

To see which way you are facing, tap the navigation arrow (bottom left) until it shows a blue beam around the blue circle.

Satellite view can also be used for the Flyover feature, or Flyover Tour, if this is available for the selected area.

Open Maps, you are here

Tap the blue circle to view details

Press and hold to drop a Pin

Satellite 3D view

Finding a route

Tap the Directions button and enter your start and end points.

Maps will calculate a route. It will also tell you how long it will take by car, public transport or by foot.

1 By default, your current location is used for the **Start** field. If you want to change this, tap and enter a new location or address

2 Enter a destination (**End**) location or address

3 Tap on the **Route** button on the keyboard (or at the top of the Directions window)

4 The route is shown on the map

5 Tap on the **Start** button to get directions

6 The route is shown on the map with directions for each section. As you follow the directions they will change for the next step of the journey

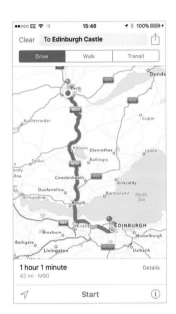

Hot tip

The Google Maps app is a good alternative that can be downloaded to your iPhone 6s. It includes voice-guided, turn-by-turn navigation, live traffic conditions and information on public transport. Google claims to constantly keep the "map of the world" updated!

News

The iPhone 6s with iOS 9 is ideal for keeping up with the news, whether you are on the move or at home. This is made even easier with the News app, which can be used to collate news stories from numerous online media outlets, covering hundreds of subjects. To use it:

1 Tap once on the **News** app

2 Tap once on the **Get Started** button

Welcome to **News**

The best stories from the sources you love, selected just for you. The more you read, the more personalized your News becomes.

News and Privacy

Get Started

After tapping on the **Get Started** button in Step 2 you will be asked if you want email alerts for the news feeds that you select. Tap on **Sign Me Up** or **Not Now**, as required.

3 Tap on news publications in which you are interested and then tap on the **Continue** button

Continue

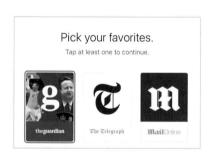

Pick your favorites.

Tap at least one to continue.

Get News in Your Inbox

The best stories, selected just for you.

Sign Me Up

Not Now

4 Items from the selected publications are displayed on the **For You** page. Tap on an item to read it in full

For You

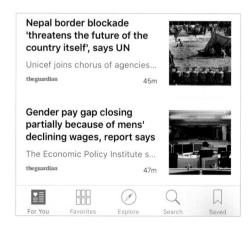

Nepal border blockade 'threatens the future of the country itself', says UN

Unicef joins chorus of agencies...

theguardian   45m

Gender pay gap closing partially because of mens' declining wages, report says

The Economic Policy Institute s...

theguardian   47m

For You   Favorites   Explore   Search   Saved

5 Tap on the **Favorites** button on the bottom toolbar to view the publications that were added in Step 3

Favorites

Don't forget

Tap on the **Edit** button to remove existing Favorite publications in Step 5.

6 Tap on the **Explore** button to add more items

Explore

7 Select more publications or specific topics, by tapping on this button. These will be available on the **For You** and **Favorites** pages

Hot tip

Tap on the **Search** button on the bottom toolbar to look for specific publications or subjects. These can then be added to your News feed and will appear under the **For You** and **Favorites** sections.

Search

8 When an article has been opened for reading, tap on this button to bookmark it, and it can then be accessed from the **Saved** button on the main toolbar

Saved

131

iBooks

The iBooks app was not previously a pre-installed app on earlier versions of the iPhone. However, it comes pre-installed with iOS 9 and can be used to download and read books on your iPhone.

Tap on the **iBooks** app icon to view your library

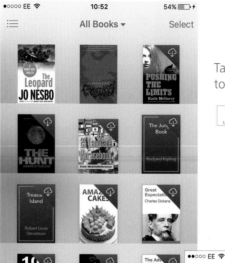

Tap on the **Featured** button to go to the iBooks Store

View, preview and download new books to read on your iPhone. These will be placed in the iBooks Library (above)

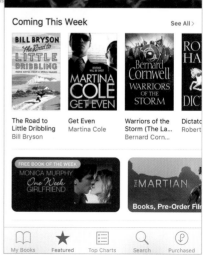

Health

The Health app in iOS 9 is designed to collect a range of health and fitness information, such as body measurements, nutrition, fitness and sleep data. It can also be used in conjunction with other health and fitness apps from the App Store and aggregate information from these too. To use the Health app:

1 Tap on this icon on the Home screen

2 Use the buttons at the bottom of the screen to access the different sections

3 Tap on the **Health Data** button to view the available categories

4 Tap on a category to view the options.
Tap on an item on each page to select it and then fill in the data as required

Hot tip

Tap on the **Add Data Point** button within a category of the Health Data section to add the data for that item.

...cont'd

5 Tap on the **Dashboard** button to view the collated information from items that you have completed in the Health Data section

Dashboard

6 Tap on the **Sources** button to view any apps that are accessing the Health app

Sources

7 Tap on the **Medical ID** button to add any important medical information such as medical conditions, blood type and allergies

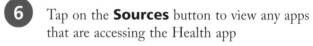

Medical ID

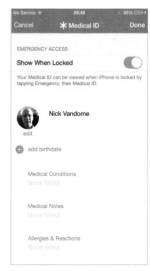

Notification Center

Although the Notification Center feature is not an app in its own right, it can be used to display information from a variety of apps. These appear as a list for all of the items you want to be reminded about or be made aware of. Notifications are set up within the Settings app. To do this:

1 Tap on the **Settings** app

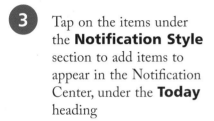

2 Tap on the **Notifications** tab

3 Tap on the items under the **Notification Style** section to add items to appear in the Notification Center, under the **Today** heading

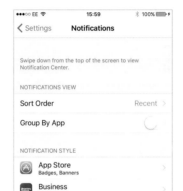

4 Drag the **Show in Notification Center** button to **On** to enable the selected app to display notifications in the Notification Center

5 Select options for the notifications sound and icon and select whether you want to show it on the Lock screen or not

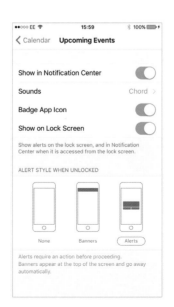

Hot tip

To enable email messages from your iCloud mail account to appear in the Notification Center, select the Mail app in Step 3 and tap on the **iCloud** button. On the next screen, drag the **Show in Notification Center** button to **On**.

...cont'd

Once the Notification Center settings have been selected, it can be used to keep up-to-date with all of your important appointments and reminders. It can also be used to display the weather for your current location. To view the Notification Center from any screen:

1 Drag down from the top of any screen to view the Notification Center. Tap on the **Today** button to view the Weather summary, Calendar items, Reminder items, stock market information and a summary of items for the next day

2 Swipe up the page to view all of the items. Tap on one to open it in its own default app

3 Tap on the **Notifications** button to view notifications from all of the selected apps in Steps 3 and 4 on the previous page

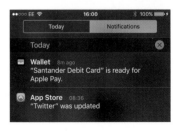

8 Working with Apps

There are thousands of apps for the iPhone, catering for every conceivable need. This chapter looks at how to find apps in the online App Store, install them, update them and remove them.

Organizing Apps

When you start downloading apps you will probably soon find that you have dozens, if not hundreds of them. You can move between screens to view all of your apps by swiping left or right with one finger.

To move an app between screens, tap and hold on it until it starts to jiggle and a cross appears in the corner. Then drag it to the side of the screen. If there is space on the next screen the app will be moved there.

As more apps are added it can become hard to find the apps you want, particularly if you have to swipe between several screens. However, it is possible to organize apps into individual folders to make using them more manageable. To do this:

1 Press on an app until it starts to jiggle and a cross appears at the top-left corner. (This can be used to delete the app unless it is a preinstalled app, in which case the cross does not appear)

2 Drag the app over another one

3 A folder is created, containing the two apps. The folder is given a default name, usually based on the category of the apps

4 Tap on the folder name and type a new name if required

Only top-level folders can be created, i.e. sub-folders cannot be created. Also, one folder cannot be placed within another.

5 Click on the **Done** button on the keyboard or the **Home** button to finish creating the folder

6 Click the **Home** button again to return to the Home screen (this is done whenever you want to return to the Home screen from an apps folder)

If you want to rename an apps folder after it has been created, tap and hold on it until it starts to jiggle. Then tap on the folder name and edit it as in Steps 4 and 5.

7 The folder is added on the Home screen. Tap on it to access the items within

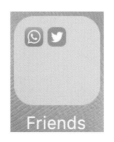

About the App Store

While the built-in apps that come with the iPhone are flexible and versatile, it really comes into its own when you connect to the App Store. This is an online resource and there are over a million apps there that can be downloaded and then used on your iPhone, including categories from Lifestyle to Travel and Medical.

To use the App Store, you must first have an Apple ID (see page 17). This can be obtained when you first connect to the App Store. Once you have an Apple ID, you can start exploring the App Store:

1 Tap on the **App Store** app on the Home screen

2 The latest available apps are displayed on the Homepage of the App Store, including the Editor's Choice, featured in the top panel

Tap on the **Categories** button to view apps in specific categories.

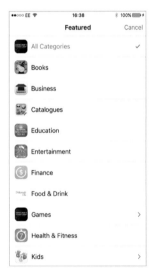

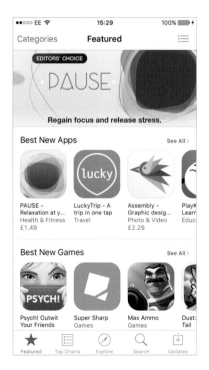

3 Tap on these buttons to view the apps according to **Featured**, **Top Charts**, **Explore** and **Updates**

Viewing apps

To view apps in the App Store and read about their content and functionality:

1 Tap once on an app

2 General details about the app are displayed

3 Swipe left or right here to view additional information about the app and view details

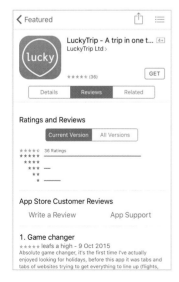

4 **Reviews** and **Related** apps are available from the relevant buttons, next to the **Details** button

Finding Apps

Featured

Within the App Store, apps are separated into categories according to type. This enables you to find apps according to particular subjects. To do this:

1 Tap on the **Featured** button on the toolbar at the bottom of the App Store

2 Swipe left and right to view items in the different category headings, e.g. Best New Apps

Don't forget

Use the **Explore** button on the bottom toolbar to find suggestions of appropriate apps based on your current geographic location.

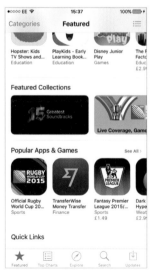

Explore

3 Scroll up the page to view additional categories and **Quick Links**

142

...cont'd

Top Charts

To find the top rated apps:

1 Tap on the **Top Charts** button on the toolbar at the bottom of the App Store

2 The top overall paid for, free and top grossing apps are displayed

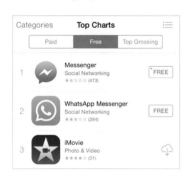

3 To find the top apps in different categories, tap on the **Categories** button

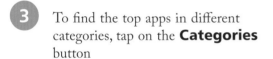

4 Select a category

5 The top apps for that category are displayed

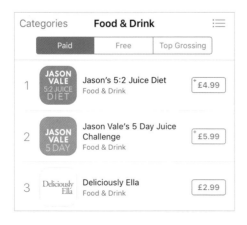

Beware

There are now so many apps, it may be difficult to find what you want. Try using the search tool and enter a word or words that describe what you are looking for.

Beware

Do not limit yourself to just viewing the top apps. Although these are the most popular, there are also a lot of excellent apps within each category.

Don't forget

Use the **Search** button on the bottom toolbar to look for specific apps using keywords.

143

Installation Process

To install apps from the App Store:

1 Find the app you want using the **App Store** on the iPhone

2 Tap the **Price** or **Free** tab

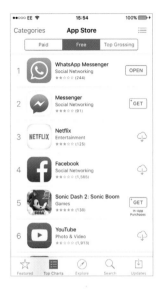

Make sure to remember your iTunes account password (your Apple ID) – you will be asked for this each time you try to install or update an app, even if it is free. Apps can also be bought using Apple Pay and Touch ID, if this is set up.

3 Tap on the **Get** button and then the **Install** button

4 If you are using Touch ID (see page 43) then this can be used to buy apps in the App Store. Enter your iTunes password, which is your Apple ID password and tap on the **OK** button

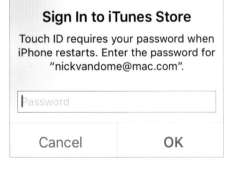

5 The app will install. After entering your password in Step 4 you can then use your Touch ID to obtain apps, or, if not, enter your Apple ID each time

Updating Apps

The publishers of apps provide updates which bring new features and improvements to your existing apps. You don't have to check your apps to see if there are updates available – you can set them to be updated automatically through the Settings app. To do this:

1 Open **Settings** and tap on the **iTunes & App Store** link

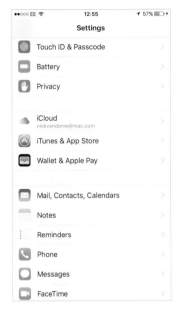

2 Drag the **Updates** button to **On** to enable automatic updates for apps

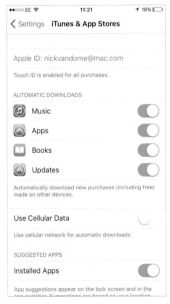

If your App Store icon has a red circle with a number inside, it means there's an update for one or more of your apps. If updates are not set to automatic, the apps can be updated manually in the **Updates** section of the App Store.

Removing Apps

To remove apps from your iPhone (excluding pre-installed ones):

1 **Press and hold** the app you want to remove

2 All the apps on the screen will start jiggling and you will see an **x** at the top of the app unless it cannot be removed, i.e. it is a pre-installed app such as Phone, Mail, Calendar, etc. (see page 19)

Don't forget

If you remove an app, it can be reinstalled from the App Store. The app will have a cloud icon next to it and will be free to reinstall, even if it was a paid-for app.

3 Tap the **x** to delete the app

4 Tap on the **Delete** button to confirm your action

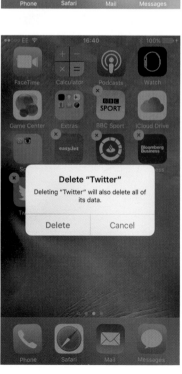

9 Web Browsing

Browsing the web on the iPhone *is very easy using* Apple's *inbuilt browser, Safari. This chapter looks at how to use Safari, navigate around web pages and save and organize bookmarks.*

Network Connections

Your iPhone can download data, such as emails and web pages, using a number of different types of connection. Some types of connection are faster than others. In general, Wi-Fi and Bluetooth should be kept off if you are not using them because they use a considerable amount of power.

GPRS
This is a slow network! But often better than nothing.

EDGE
This is a relatively slow connection but is fine for email.

3G and 4G
These are faster connections than EDGE. 4G is pretty close to Wi-Fi speed.

Wi-Fi connection
Joining a wireless connection will give you fairly fast download speeds. There are many free Wi-Fi hotspots. You can use home Wi-Fi once you enter the password.

Bluetooth
This is a short-range wireless connection, generally used for communication using a Bluetooth headset.

What do the various icons mean?
Look at the top of the iPhone and you will see various icons relating to cellular and other networks.

●●●●○	Signal strength
O2-UK	Network provider
📶	Wi-Fi On, with good signal strength
✳	Bluetooth On
✈	Airplane mode On
⁂	iPhone is busy connecting, getting mail, or another task which has not completed

Wi-Fi and Bluetooth drain battery power. Switch off when not required.

Configuring Networks

Wi-Fi

1 Go to **Settings > Wi-Fi**

2 Tap **On** if it is off

3 Choose a **network** from those listed and enter the password

4 Tap **Ask to Join Networks** if you want to be prompted each time a new network is found. It's generally easier to leave this **Off**

5 If you want to forget the network (e.g. maybe you have used one in a hotel), tap the name of the network you have joined, and tap **Forget This Network**

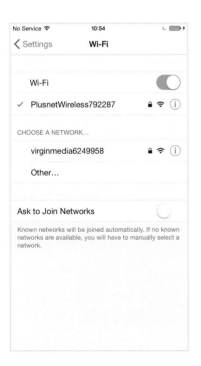

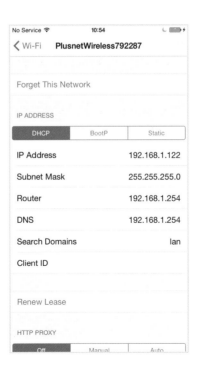

Browse with Safari

The Safari app is the default web browser on the iPhone. This can be used to view web pages, save favorites and read pages with the Reader function. To start using Safari:

1 Tap on the **Safari** app

When a page loads in Safari a blue status bar underneath the page name indicates the progress of the loading page.

2 Tap on the Address Bar at the top of the Safari window. Type a web page address

3 Tap on the **Go** button on the keyboard to open the web page

Go

Scroll up to the top of the page to activate the top address bar, and the bottom toolbar when you tap on the page.

4 Or, suggested options appear as you type. Tap on one of these to go to that page

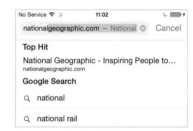

5 The selected web page opens in Safari

Tap the time at the top of the screen to move to the top of the web page (this works with text messages, and other apps like Facebook, too). This is called Fast Scrolling.

6 Swipe up and down and left and right to navigate around the page

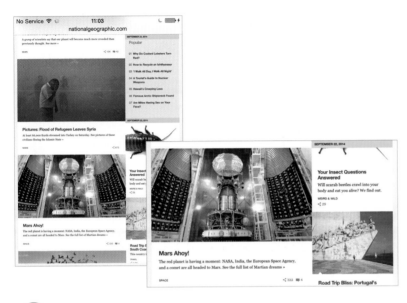

7 With thumb and forefinger, spread outwards to zoom in on a web page (pinch inwards to zoom back out)

Don't forget

Double-tap with one finger to zoom in on a page by a set amount. Double-tap with one finger to return to normal view. If the page has been zoomed by a greater amount by pinching, double-tap with two fingers to return to normal view.

Don't forget

You can also zoom in by placing your thumb and forefinger on the screen and pushing them apart (pinch them inwards to zoom out again).

Hot tip

You don't have to type ".com" or ".co.uk" for website addresses – simply hold down the "period" key and alternatives will pop up.

151

Navigating Pages

When you are viewing pages within Safari there are a number of functions that can be used:

1 Tap on these buttons to move forward and back between web pages that have been visited

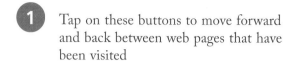

2 Tap here to view Bookmarked pages, Reading List pages and Shared Links

3 Tap here to add a bookmark, add to a reading list, add to a note, add an icon to your iPhone Home screen, email a link to a page, Tweet a page, send it to Facebook or print a page

4 Tap here to add a new tab (see page 154)

5 Tap on a link on a page to open it. Tap and hold to access additional options, to open in a new tab, add to a Reading List or copy the link

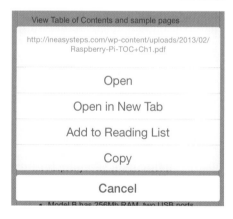

6 Tap and hold on an image and tap on **Save Image** or **Copy**

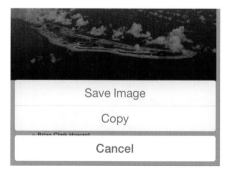

Hot tip

Tap and hold on the **Forward** and **Back** buttons to view lists of previously-visited pages in these directions.

Hot tip

If a web page has this button in the Address bar/ Smart Search box it means that the page can be viewed with the **Reader** function. This displays the page as text only, without any of the accompanying design to distract from the content. Tap on the button so that it turns black to activate the Reader.

Add Web Clips to the Home Screen

If you find a site that you want to revisit, but not add to bookmarks, you can add it to the Home screen:

1 Open the required web page

Hot tip

Add regularly-visited websites to your Home screen to save you having to look for the bookmark.

2 Tap on the **Share** button and tap on the **Add to Home Screen** button

3 Give the page a name and tap on the **Add** button

4 The web clip is added to the Home screen as an icon

Opening New Tabs

Safari supports tabbed browsing, which means that you can open separate pages within the same window and access them by tapping on each tab at the top of the page:

1 Tap here to view the open tabs

Tap on the **Private** button in the tabs window to open a Private browsing session, where no web details will be recorded.

2 The open tabs are displayed. Tap on one to go to that tab

3 Tap on this button at the bottom of the window to create a new tab

4 Tap on the cross on a tab to close it

5 Open a new tab as in Step 3, entering a web address into the Address Bar, or tap on one of the thumbnails in the **Favorites** window

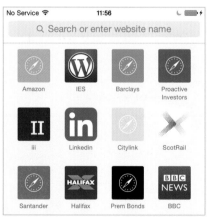

The items that appear in the Favorites window can be determined within **Settings > Safari** and tapping once on the **Favorites** link.

154

Bookmarking Pages

Once you start using Safari you will soon build up a collection of favorite pages that you visit regularly. To access these quickly they can be bookmarked so that you can then go to them in one tap. To set up and use bookmarks:

1 Open a web page that you want to bookmark. Tap here to access the sharing options

2 Tap on the **Add Bookmark** button

3 Tap on this link and select whether to include the bookmark on the Favorites Bar or in a Bookmarks folder

4 Tap on the **Save** button

5 Tap on the **Bookmarks** button

6 Tap here on the **Bookmarks** button to view all of the bookmarks. The Bookmarks folders are listed. Tap on the **Edit** button to delete or rename the folders

Reading List and Shared Links

The button in Step 5 on the previous page can also be used to access your Reading List and Shared Links.

Reading List

This is a list of web pages that have been saved for reading at a later date. The great thing about this function is that the pages can be read even when you are offline and not connected to the internet.

Don't forget

Reading List items can be added from the Share button in Step 1 on the previous page.

1 Tap on this button to view your **Reading List**

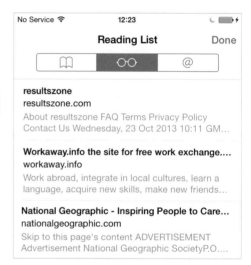

Shared Links

If you have added a Twitter account on your iPhone you will be able to view your updates from the Shared Links button.

Hot tip

If you have accounts with Facebook or Twitter, you can link to these from their own headings within the **Settings** app. Once you have done this you can share content to these sites from apps on your iPhone.

1 Tap on this button to view your **Shared Links** updates

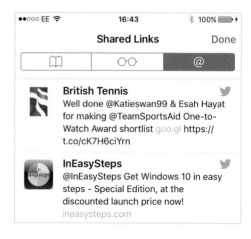

Safari Settings

Settings for Safari can be specified in the Settings app. To do this:

1 Tap on the **Settings** app

2 Tap on the **Safari** tab

3 Tap on the **Search Engine** link to select a default search engine to use

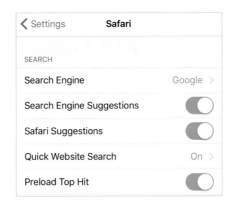

< Settings	**Safari**
SEARCH	
Search Engine	Google >
Search Engine Suggestions	
Safari Suggestions	
Quick Website Search	On >
Preload Top Hit	

4 Tap on the default search engine you want to use with Safari, and return to Settings

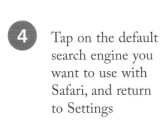

Beware

Don't use **Autofill** for names and passwords on any sites with sensitive information, such as banking sites, if other people have access to your iPhone.

5 Tap here for options for filling in online forms

Passwords	>
AutoFill	>

6 Tap on this button to access options for opening new links on a web site

Open Links	In New Tab >

7 Tap on this button to access options for the Favorites window that appears when you open a new tab

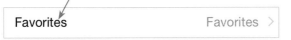

Favorites	Favorites >

...cont'd

8 Drag the **Do Not Track** button to **Off** to disable this. If tracking is Off then no information will be recorded about visited websites

PRIVACY & SECURITY

Do Not Track

Block Cookies   Allow from Websites I Visit   >

9 Tap on the **Block Cookies** link to specify how Safari deals with cookies from websites

10 Tap on **Clear History and Website Data** to remove these items

Clear History and Website Data

11 Drag this button to **On** to enable alerts for when you are about to visit a fraudulent website

Fraudulent Website Warning

12 Drag this button to **On** to block pop-up messages

Block Pop-ups

Cookies are small items from websites that obtain details from your browser when you visit a site. The cookie remembers the details for the next time you visit the site.

If the **History and Website Data** is cleared then there will be no record of any sites that have been visited.

10 Email

Most of us spend a great deal of time reading and composing emails. This chapter looks at how to set up email on your iPhone *so that you can send and receive emails with your friends, family and colleagues.*

Setting Up Email

The iPhone handles email well, and works with iCloud and Microsoft Exchange. It handles POP3, IMAP and can work with Yahoo! Mail, Google Mail and AOL.

Setting up an email account

You can link to a variety of email accounts on the iPhone. This example uses a Gmail account:

The iPhone can handle many types of email account. IMAP accounts are useful since you can see all your folders on the server, and can save email to specific folders easily.

1 Go to **Settings > Mail, Contacts, Calendars**

2 Tap on the **Add Account** button

3 Select the account you want to add (in this case Google)

If you set up an iCloud account you will automatically be given an iCloud email account.

4 Enter the account details and tap on the **Next** button

5 Select the items you want to include in the account and tap on the **Save** button

Deleting an account

To delete an email account from your iPhone:

1 Go to **Settings > Mail, Contacts, Calendars**

2 Tap on the account you want to delete

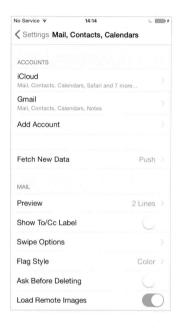

3 In the account window, swipe down to the bottom of the screen and tap on the **Delete Account** button and then the **Delete from My iPhone** button

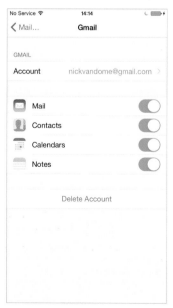

Using Exchange Server

Mail can collect email, and sync calendars and contacts using Microsoft Exchange Server, which is great news for businesses. To do this:

1 Go to **Settings > Mail, Contacts, Calendars**

2 Tap on the **Exchange** button

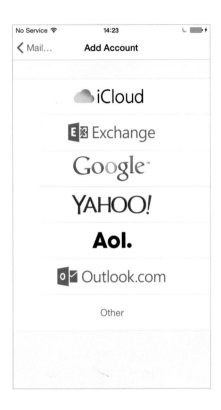

3 Enter the details of your Exchange account (you may need to get these from your IT Administrator) and tap on the **Next** button

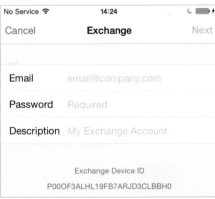

Email Viewing Settings

As with other apps, there are a number of settings for email:

1 Go to **Settings > Mail, Contacts, Calendars**

2 Tap on one of the accounts to view its settings

3 Adjust settings for **Preview**, **Ask Before Deleting**, **Show To/Cc Label**, etc.

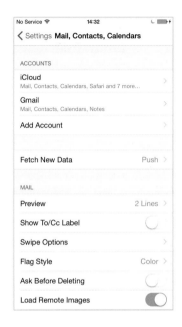

4 Access **Settings > General > Accessibility > Larger Text** to change the text size

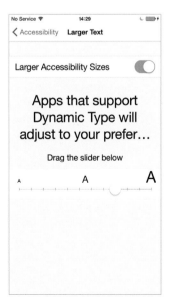

Hot tip

If you want to see more text on the screen set the font size to small.

Composing Email

You can keep in touch with everyone, straight from the Mail app:

1 Tap the **Mail** icon to open the app

2 Tap an **email account** to open it

3 Tap the **New Email** icon (bottom right). A new email will open

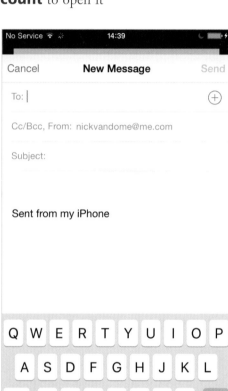

4 Tap the **To:** field and type the name of the recipient

5 Tap the **Subject:** and enter a subject for the email

6 Tap the **email body** area (below Subject:) and start typing your email

7 Insert a photo by pressing and holding in the body of the email and selecting **Insert Photo or Video** from the pop-up menu and then select a photo from your photo gallery

8 Once complete, hit **Send**

Hot tip

To add documents to emails, press on the subject area of the email and select **Add Attachment** from the pop-up menu. Select the required document from within the iCloud Drive and click on the **Done** button.

Reading Email

When you receive email you can view it in the Mail app:

1   Check the **Mail** icon for fresh mail – represented by a red circle. The number refers to the number of unread emails

2   Tap **Mail** to open

3   Tap the **Inbox** to access the email, and if there is blue dot next to an email it means that it is unread

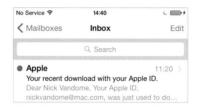

4   If there is an attachment for the email this will be indicated by a paperclip icon next to it – you can tap to download

5   The attachment will appear in the body of the email. Tap on it to download it within the email

6   When the image attachment has finished downloading it will be visible in the body of the email

Flag important emails so you can find them again easily. Swipe from right to left on the email and tap on the **Flag** button.

Often, attachments do not download automatically. Tap the icon and you will see the attachment downloading. After downloading, tap to open.

To save documents, tap on the Share button and then tap on the relevant app to save within it, e.g. iBooks (to save PDFs), etc. To save a photo from an email, press and hold on the photo until you see **Save Image**. Tap on this, and the photo will be added to the **Photos** section of the **Photos** app.

Forwarding Email

Once you have received an email you can reply to the sender, or forward it to someone else:

1 Open an email

2 Tap the **Reply/ Forward** icon at the bottom right of the screen

Double-check that you have selected the correct button when forwarding an email, in case you are making comments about the original sender and accidentally **Reply** to them, rather than **Forward** to a new recipient.

3 Select **Forward**

4 Enter the name of the recipient in the **To:** box

5 In the body of the email, enter any message you want to accompany the forwarded email

6 Tap on the **Send** button

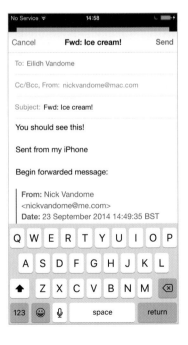

Deleting Email

You can delete email in a couple of different ways

1 Tap the email to read it

2 When finished, tap the trash icon at the bottom of the screen

Alternative method

1 In the email list view, slide your finger across the email from right to left (do not open it)

2 A red **Trash** box should appear

3 Tap **Trash** and the email will be deleted

Yet another way of deleting email is

1 Go to **Inbox** and tap the **Edit** button at the top right

2 The contents of the Inbox are displayed in Edit mode

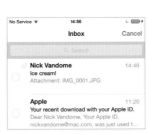

3 Tap each email you want to delete and a blue circle will appear in the left column

4 Hit **Trash**, in the bottom right-hand corner, when you are ready to delete

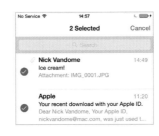

Hot tip

There are also options in the slide feature to **Flag** the email and a **More** button, from which you can reply, forward, mark or move the email.

Moving Email to Folders

If you have an IMAP account, such as an iCloud account, you can see your folders on the server. You can move mail from your Inbox to another folder. This helps keep your mail organized, and your Inbox uncluttered.

1 Open the email you want to move, and tap on the **Folder** button on the bottom toolbar

Hot tip

Avoid having an Inbox full of read and new mail. Move items to folders (easy with IMAP accounts) or delete them.

168

2 Tap on the folder into which you want to move the email. In this instance, it is **Family**

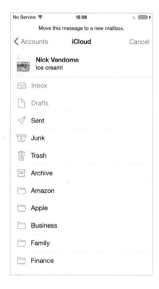

3 The email appears in the selected folder

11 Accessibility Settings

The iPhone *is well suited for people with visual or motor issues. This chapter details the Accessibility options on the* iPhone, *so that everyone can get the most out of it.*

Accessibility Settings

Many people with visual, hearing or motor issues should be able to make use of devices like the iPhone. With the standard default configuration they may run into problems, but the iPhone has many settings that can be modified to make them more usable.

What features are available?

- VoiceOver

- Zoom

- White on Black

- Mono Audio

- Speak Auto-text

Most of these features will work with most applications, apart from VoiceOver which will only work with the iPhone's standard (pre-installed) applications.

1 Tap on the **Settings** app

2 Tap on the **General** tab

3 Tap on the **Accessibility** link

4 The **Accessibility** options are displayed – tap on a link to access more options

5 Or, drag the button **On** or **Off** to access these

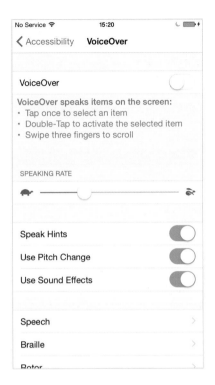

6 Swipe up and down the page to view the full range of options for each item

Activate Settings on the iPhone

Switching on VoiceOver

1 Go to **Settings > General > Accessibility**

2 Activate **VoiceOver** as shown below

3 When finished, you may wish to switch it off again

Tap on VoiceOver and drag the button on to activate it

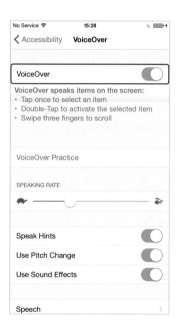

Switch to Zoom to enlarge (Zoom cannot be used with VoiceOver)

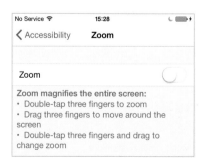

VoiceOver

VoiceOver

This speaks what's on the screen, so you can tell what's on the screen even if you cannot see it. It describes items on the screen and, if text is selected, VoiceOver will read the text.

Speaking rate

This can be adjusted using the settings.

Typing feedback

VoiceOver can provide this: go to **Settings > General > Accessibility > VoiceOver > Typing Feedback**.

Languages

VoiceOver is available in languages other than English (but is not available in all languages).

VoiceOver Gestures

When VoiceOver is active, the standard touchscreen gestures operate differently:

Tap	Speak item
Flick right or left	Select next or previous item
Flick up or down	Depends on Rotor Control setting
Two-finger tap	Stop speaking current item
Two-finger flick up	Read all from top of screen
Two-finger flick down	Read all from current position
Three-finger flick up or down	Scroll one page at a time
Three-finger flick right or left	Go to next or previous page
Three-finger tap	Speak the scroll status

Apple Support for VoiceOver

See: **http://support.apple.com/kb/HT3598**

Zoom

The iPhone touchscreen lets you zoom in and out of elements on the screen. Zoom will let you magnify the whole screen, irrespective of which application you are running.

Turn Zoom on and off

1 Go to **Settings > General > Accessibility > Zoom**

2 Tap the Zoom **Off/On** switch

3 You cannot use Zoom and VoiceOver at the same time

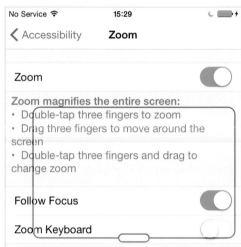

To increase the overall text size on your iPhone, select **Settings > Accessibility > Larger Text**.

Zoom in and out

1 Double tap the screen with three fingers

2 The screen will then magnify by 200%

Working with magnification

1 Double-tap with **three fingers** and drag to the top of the zoom window (increase magnification) or bottom (decrease magnification)

2 Drag with **three fingers** to move around the zoom window

Other Accessibility Settings

Activate Increase Contrast

This feature enhances the contrast on the iPhone, which may make it easier for some people to read.

1 Go to **Settings > General > Accessibility**

2 Tap the **Increase Contrast** link

3 Drag the **Reduce Transparency** button to **On**

Turn Mono Audio on and off

This combines the sound of both left and right channels into a mono audio signal played through both sides.

1 Go to **Settings > General > Accessibility**

2 Switch On **Mono Audio**

Turn Speak Auto-text on

This setting enables the iPhone to speak text corrections and suggestions as you type text into the iPhone.

1 Go to **Settings > General > Accessibility**

2 Select **Speech** and switch On **Speak Auto-text**

3 Speak Auto-text works with both VoiceOver and Zoom

Large phone keypad

The keypad of the iPhone is large, making it easy for people who are visually impaired to see the digits.

1 Tap the **Phone** icon (on the dock)

2 Tap the **Keypad** icon (4th icon from left)

Closed Captioning (**Settings > General > Accessibility > Subtitles & Captioning** (under Media) > **Closed Captions + SDH**) adds subtitles to video content. Not all videos contain Closed Captioning information but where it is available you can access it by turning on Closed Captions.

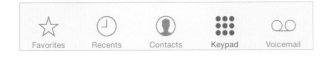

Restrictions

If children are going to be using your iPhone, or if they have their own, you may want to restrict the type of content they can access:

1 Tap on the **Settings** app

2 Tap on the **General** tab

3 Tap on the **Restrictions** link

4 By default, the restrictions are disabled, i.e. grayed-out, so they cannot be accessed. Tap on the **Enable Restrictions** button

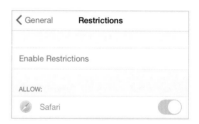

5 Set a passcode in order to set restrictions

Beware

If you are restricting items for someone, make sure that you discuss it with them and explain your reasons for doing this, rather than just letting them find out for themselves when they try to use an app.

6 For the items you want to restrict, drag their buttons to **Off**. These icons will no longer appear on the iPhone's Home screen

12 Solving Problems

The iPhone *occasionally misbehaves — an* app *will not close, or the* iPhone *may malfunction. This section looks at how to fix common problems and provides some helpful websites. The chapter also helps you find your lost or stolen* iPhone.

General iPhone Care

The iPhone is a fairly robust gadget but, like any complex piece of electronic hardware, it may suffer from knocks, scratches, getting wet and other problems.

Cleaning the body and screen

The touchscreen is supposed to be scratch resistant. In fact, there are YouTube videos showing people trying to scratch the screen by placing the iPhone into a plastic bag containing keys and shaking the whole thing around. Amazingly, the screen seems to not get scratched. Then they put it in a blender and it, well, got blended. So it's definitely not blender-proof!

Hot tip

Paper kitchen towel, dampened with a little water containing a couple of drops of dishwashing liquid, is great for getting rid of heavily greased screens.

The best way to clean an iPhone is with a lint-free cloth such as the one above used for cleaning reading glasses. Make sure there is no grit or sand on the body or screen and gently rub with the cleaning cloth. This should bring back the shine without scratching the glass or the body of the phone.

Occasionally the screen may get very greasy and a little soap helps to get the grease off

Hot tip

A glass protector is an excellent option for the iPhone screen.

1. Put a few drops of dishwashing liquid in warm water

2. Get some paper kitchen towel and dip this into the water

3. Wring out the kitchen towel so it is not dripping wet and lightly wipe over the screen and rest of the casing

4. Dry off using a clean cloth

Keep the iPhone Up-to-Date

Apple releases updates to the iPhone operating system periodically.

Is your iPhone fully up-to-date?

1. Tap on the **Settings** app

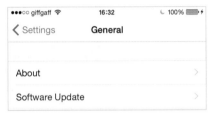

2. Tap on the **General** tab

General

3. Tap on the **Software Update** link to view the current status of your operating system

●●●○○ giffgaff 🔵   16:32   🔋 100% 🔋⚡

‹ Settings   **General**

About   ›

Software Update   ›

4. If there is an update available it will be displayed

5. Tap on the **Download and Install** button

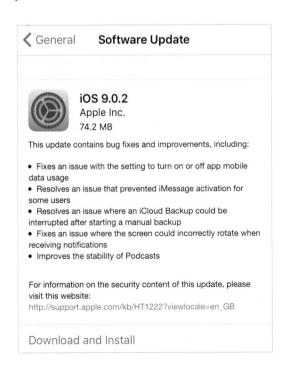

‹ General   **Software Update**

iOS 9.0.2
Apple Inc.
74.2 MB

This update contains bug fixes and improvements, including:

- Fixes an issue with the setting to turn on or off app mobile data usage
- Resolves an issue that prevented iMessage activation for some users
- Resolves an issue where an iCloud Backup could be interrupted after starting a manual backup
- Fixes an issue where the screen could incorrectly rotate when receiving notifications
- Improves the stability of Podcasts

For information on the security content of this update, please visit this website:
http://support.apple.com/kb/HT1222?viewlocale=en_GB

Download and Install

Don't forget

Software updates for iPhone users are provided free by Apple. If one becomes available, download and install it.

Maximize the iPhone Battery

The iPhone is a bit of a power hog. Browsing the web, listening to music and watching videos drains significant amounts of power. If you only make a few phone calls each day, your iPhone will last a couple of days between charges. But most people use it for far more than this, and their battery will last about a day.

Tweaks to ensure maximum battery life

You can conserve battery power by switching off Wi-Fi and Bluetooth. Instead of opting for push email, you can check for email manually.

Consider using Airplane Mode (**Settings > Airplane Mode**) for conservation of power. However, you will not be able to make or receive any calls, texts or notifications.

1 Switch Off **Wi-Fi** if you don't need it

2 Switch Off **Bluetooth** if you don't need it

3 Switch On the **Battery Percentage** indicator, under **Settings > Battery**

4 Use a lower cellular speed, e.g. 3G instead of 4G under **Settings > Cellular** (**Mobile**) **> Voice & Data**

5 Collect your **email manually**, under **Mail, Contacts, Calendars > Fetch New Data**

6 Set **Auto-lock** to a short period, e.g. 1 minute, under **Settings > General > Auto-Lock**

7 Reduce the brightness of your screen, under **Settings > Display & Brightness**

The display brightness can also be altered from within the Control Center (swipe up from the bottom of the screen).

8 Press the **Off** button once when you have finished using the iPhone (this is Sleep mode which uses less power)

Restart, Force Quit and Reset

Restart the iPhone

If the iPhone freezes, or applications act strangely, you can restart the iPhone.

1 **Hold down** the **On/Off** button

2 When you see the **Slide to Power Off** appear, **swipe this to the right**

3 Leave the iPhone for a couple of minutes then press the **On/Off** button again and let the phone restart

Don't forget

The On/Off button is also used for the Sleep/Wake function.

Quit an app

Sometimes apps freeze or misbehave and you'll want to quit and reopen them. To do this:

1 Press the Home button twice to access the multitasking window

2 Swipe left or right to find the app that you want to quit and swipe it up to the top of the screen

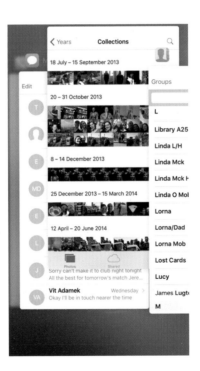

Force Quit the iPhone

1 Press the **On/Off** and the **Home button** at the same time

2 The screen will suddenly turn black and the iPhone will automatically restart

...cont'd

Resetting the iPhone

There are various aspects of your iPhone that can be reset to their factory defaults. These include resetting the Home screen layout, network settings and the keyboard dictionary. You can also reset all of the settings on the iPhone, or erase the content and settings. This erases all of the content and resets the iPhone to its factory, unused, condition. You may want to do this if you have been using the iPhone and then want to give it to someone else. To do this:

The **Reset Home Screen Layout** option returns your Home screen to the way it was when you first got your iPhone.

1 Select **Settings > General** and tap on the **Reset** button (at the bottom of the page)

Reset	>

2 All of the Reset options are displayed. Tap on the **Erase All Content and Settings** button

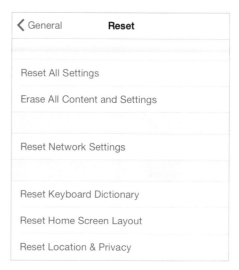

‹ General   **Reset**

Reset All Settings

Erase All Content and Settings

Reset Network Settings

Reset Keyboard Dictionary

Reset Home Screen Layout

Reset Location & Privacy

3 Enter the passcode if you use one to lock your iPhone

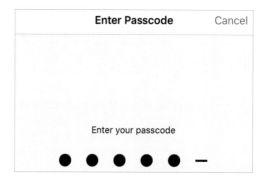

Enter Passcode   Cancel

Enter your passcode

● ● ● ● ● —

4 Tap on the **Erase iPhone** button

This will delete all media and data, and reset all settings.

Erase iPhone

Cancel

5 Since it is a serious action, you will be asked if you are sure. Tap on the **Erase iPhone** button again

Are you sure you want to continue? All media, data, and settings will be erased.
This cannot be undone.

Erase iPhone

Cancel

6 Enter your Apple ID and tap on the **Erase** button to return your iPhone to its factory condition

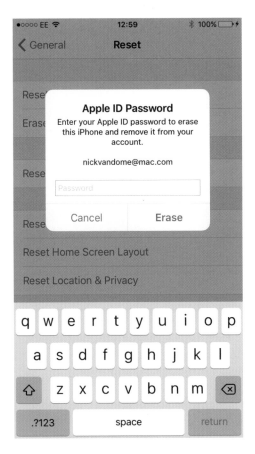

●○○○○ EE 📶   12:59   ☀ 100% 🔋⚡

‹ General   **Reset**

Rese

Erase

Apple ID Password

Enter your Apple ID password to erase this iPhone and remove it from your account.

nickvandome@mac.com

Password

Cancel   Erase

Rese

Reset Home Screen Layout

Reset Location & Privacy

Hot tip

If you reset the contents and settings for your iPhone you can restore them when you next turn on the phone. This can be done from an iCloud or an iTunes backup and is done at the **Set Up iPhone** step of the setup process.

183

Apple Resources

Visit Apple!

The first place you should look for help is the Apple site. After all, the iPhone is their creation so they should know more about it than anyone.

The iPhone and iPhone Support areas are packed with information, tutorials and videos.

Useful URLs

http://www.apple.com/iphone/

http://www.apple.com/support/iphone/

David Pogue's posts

David Pogue is always worth reading – he loves technology and loves all things Apple. Try his own website at:

http://davidpogue.com/

iLounge.com

iLounge has long provided loads of hints and tips for Apple devices. These guys review hardware, accessories and provide reviews of new gear for the iPhone, the iPad and the iPod.

I Use This (iphone.iusethis.com)

Provides reviews of iPhone apps, and lets you know how many people are actually using the apps.

What's on iPhone (whatsoniphone.com)

Largely a review site but it also provides information about hardware and for people interested in developing for the iPhone.

The first place to look for hints, tips and fixes, if you can't find them within this book, is Apple's website, which is chock full of information and videos.

If You Lose Your iPhone

If you have lost or misplaced your iPhone, you can use iCloud to look for its location. The iPhone has to be on and transmitting to the cellular network in order for Find My iPhone to work.

Find My iPhone also allows you to erase the entire contents of your iPhone remotely. This means that if it gets stolen, you can remotely erase the iPhone and prevent whoever stole your iPhone from getting their hands on your personal data.

Set up Find My iPhone

Before you use Find My iPhone it has to be set up. To do this:

1 Within **Settings** tap on the **iCloud** tab

2 Tap on the **Find My iPhone** link and if the **Find My iPhone** functionality is Off, drag the button to **On**

Hot tip

If for no other reason, it is worth getting an iCloud account so you can track your iPhone and erase the contents if it gets stolen.

185

3 Tap on the **Allow** button in the Find My iPhone dialog box to activate this functionality

Find My iPhone

This enables Find My iPhone features, including the ability to show the location of this iPhone on a map.

Cancel | Allow

Locating your iPhone

Once you have set up Find My iPhone, you can then use the online service to locate it, lock it, or erase its contents.

1 **Log in to iCloud** (**www. icloud.com**) from a PC or other Apple device

2 Click on the **Find My iPhone** button

...cont'd

The **Play Sound** option is a good one if you have lost the iPhone in your own home.

If you are using Apple Pay, this will be deactivated if you click on the **Lost Mode** button in Step 6. This is a good security measure if you lose your iPhone.

Click on the **Erase iPhone > Erase** button if you are worried that someone might compromise the data on your iPhone.

3 To use the Find My iPhone functionality you have to sign in again with your Apple ID

4 The location of your iPhone is shown on a map

5 Click on the **i** symbol to see options for your lost iPhone

6 Details about the phone, and options for what you can do, are displayed

7 Click on the **Play Sound** button to send an alert sound to the phone. A message is displayed to let you know that a sound has been sent to your iPhone

8 Click on the **Lost Mode** button to lock your iPhone remotely. You have to enter a passcode to do this and this will be required to unlock the iPhone

Index

D

E

F

G